Ayodhya Ram Temple and Hindu Renaissance

BY THE SAME AUTHOR

Economic Development and Reforms in India and China

Hindus Under Siege: The Way Out

Sri Lanka in Crisis: India's Options

Terrorism in India: A Strategy of Deterrence for India's National Security

Rama Setu: Symbol of National Unity

Corruption and Corporate Governance in India: Satyam, Spectrum and Sundaram

Hindutva and National Renaissance

India's China Strategic Perspective

Virat Hindu Identity: Concept and its Power

Building the Sri Rama Temple in Ayodhya

2G Spectrum Scam

The Ideology of India's Modern Right

Ayodhya Ram Temple and Hindu Renaissance

Subramanian Swamy, Ph.D. (Harvard)

Member of Parliament, India
Former Union Cabinet Minister for
Commerce, Law & Justice, India

Satya Paul Sabharwal

HAR-ANAND
PUBLICATIONS PVT LTD

Reprint, 2024

Published by Ashok Gosain and Ashish Gosain for:
HAR-ANAND PUBLICATIONS PVT LTD
E-49/3, Okhla Industrial Area, Phase-II, New Delhi-110020
Tel: 41603490
E-mail: info@haranandbooks.com/haranand@rediffmail.com
Shop online at: www.haranandbooks.com

@haranand_publications
Har Anand Publications

Printed in India

Preface

India, that is Bharat, and also known as Hindustan, has survived over 900 years of foreign oppression: first by the brutal foreign aggression of Islam and then by subversion of our national mindset by foreign Christian forces compounded by loot, cruel debilitating intrusive religious conversions, finally in 1947 India overthrow foreign occupation and rule to emerge as a democratic Republic of India.

Since then India has recovered substantially, remained democratic, and survived five wars, suppressed secession attempts, and has now emerged as the third most prosperous country and second most populous nation in the world.

Today in 2020, India is at a turning point in history and the question arises whether or not it can emerge as an innovative global economic and military power with a population whose mental outlook/mindset, matches the requirements of this global role objective.

The answer is: India must do so, for the sake of global survival and stability in this 21st century. Whether we will rise to this commitment will depend on the appropriate commensurate mindset development of our people. The question is how to structure that mindset development.

The overwhelming majority of India's population is the Brihad Hindu community (see Explanation II in Article 25 of the Constitution of India)—consisting of Sanatana Dharmis,

Buddhists, Jains and Sikhs, that is about 82.5 per cent of the total Indian population.

India's religious minorities are constituted by Muslims (13 per cent), Christians (2.5 per cent) and some other small religious groups. Though Buddhists, Jains and Sikhs are also considered religious minorities, they are really so close to the majority Sanatana Dharma community in culture and indigenous ancestry that they are considered as partners in Hindu society.

Unlike Islam and Christianity, these other minority religions were born as dissenting theologies of Hinduism. They share the core concepts with Hindus such as re-incarnation, equality of all religions, and ability to meet God in this life.

That these dissenting theologies feel somewhat alienated from Hindu society nowadays, is the consequence of India's identity crisis created by disinformation. The ideology of the Modern Right in India today seeks to end this identity crisis and bring about a renaissance in our national culture.

For achieving this national renaissance, we require an ideological framework of the Modern Right, which we propose to articulate and propagate in this book, in an intellectually challenging way, it has the following markers:

(*a*) A social ethos, termed Hindutva or "Hinduness", based on the Hindu concepts of harmonious secularism, trusteeship of wealth, philanthropy, and voluntary group self-help, for better quality of life, and for minimizing economic contradictions and deprivation.

(*b*) A state which is Hindutva flavored, based on the present Indian Constitution, minimalist in regulatory interventions in social and economic matters, maximalist in the maintenance of law and order and equality in gender development, and in crushing social obscurantism and in a governance, which is politically accountable to the people in the framework of egalitarian democracy.

(*c*) Empowerment of the individual through a modern and accessible education that blends the essential concepts of spiritual commitment of Hindutva, with pursuit of material goals, to enable the individual to be self-reliant, capable of rational risk taking, and have the strong moral character-basedtime-tested values of Hindutva. The religious minorities are protected in core freedoms and fundamental rights by the Constitution but it is stressed that they are genetically of the same Hindu ancestry.

(*d*) Actions of the State shall be restricted to, and promised largely by incentives, and with reasonable exceptions, they shall never be coercion. The State should make no such promise to the people without specifying the sacrifice to be made for meeting the promise.

(*e*) India's rapid economic progress must be with the goal to become an advanced developed country, as a globally competitive economy requiring assured access to the markets and technological innovations of the developed countries.

(*f*) A national security strategy for a peaceful environment which requires strong security ties with such of those countries with which India has no intrinsic and immutable clash of interests and harmonization in relations with, and close cultural and economic relations.

These goals can be attained by developing a strong and coherent ideology of the Modern Right, based on the concept of Hindutva national identity—whose defining characteristics can be culled from a correct perception of our history.

To propagate this new ideology, the Virat Hindustan Sangam was founded in 2014 (www.vhsindia.org). This book however is focused on re-building the Sri Rama Temple at Ayodhya as a stepping stone in the path to create a renaissance in India that is Bharat, as a Virat Hindustan.

1 January 2020

SUBRAMANIAN SWAMY
SATYA PAUL SABHARWAL

ADDENDUM PREFACE

कर्मण्येवाधिकारस्तेमाफलेषुकदाचन /
माकर्मफलहेतुर्भूर्मातेसङ्गोऽस्त्वकर्मणि ||2.47||

Enthused and driven by Dr. Subramanian Swamy's teaching adopted and enshrined in 47 Padh of 2nd Adhyay of Bhagwad Gita (i.e. just concentrating on the deed and/or actions rather than result of the same.) I remember, while going to High Court of Andhra Pradesh at Amravati where I was going for issuing of notice in freeing Tirumala Tirupati and other Hindu temples from Government control I asked Dr. Swamy "Sir, how come you are so relaxed and tension free?" He said "Satya, I'm only concerned with my actions and not with the result/fruits. The result I leave to the Lord to decide. He has his own ways of getting work done. This is why I am never nervous, tensed or scared of anything."

As an intern and later part of his Legal-eagles' team, I have always been encouraged, cheered and guided by Dr. Swamy. He always told me not to keep any blocks in mind while putting my point across. Even if, my point was not relevant, he explained and told me the corrected path. A strong believer in the Gurukul style of teachings, Dr. Swamy, made me sit with him for hours and explained his arguments and blessed me with required essentials thereof. His teachings are not only restricted to law, but also pertain to life and the way one should act, execute and look at things in life. Dr. Swamy helped me inculcate many bright thoughts and an approach to always be fearless in doing something which is correct and honest in nature. The zeal to work for Society and betterment of the Society; whether it is fighting corruption, or prosecuting the corrupt(s), saving Ram-Setu from demolition, initiating a speedy trial [day-to-day] to build the Ram Temple at Ayodhya and now, Kashi Vishwanath and Mathura is imbedded in him which I try to comprehend and inculcate. Working with him, is wholly a special system to be part of. The multi-tasking aptitude and ability of sir to work on twenty different cases, leading Politics and academics i.e. writing books and papers; and excelling in all the above is no-ordinary job. Amazed by his constant and unparalleled dedication, it is an honor for me to Co-Author this Manuscript with him.

I would like to thank Dr. Roxna Subramanian Swamy, for her indefatigable effort to sit with me on various subjects with respect to the book and explain me concepts and models. Also, I would like to thank Ma'am for her support and approval to let me use her wide-range of books, study and research for this manuscript.

1 January 2020 SATYA PAUL SABHARWAL

Contents

CHAPTER 1

Hindu Renaissance and Hindutva

Building a Ram Temple at the site in Ayodhya where their faith makes Hindu hold that Bhagwan Ram was born, constitutes a part of Hindutva. Hindutva is the quality of being a Hindu, namely "Hinduness" of a person's norms and beliefs, as well as the code of good behavior and civility, attributes that would qualify and distinguish a Hindu from others. Thus, Maryada Purushottam Bhagwan Ram is venerated as the embodiment of this eminence.

India, that is Bharat, is the name of the Indian Republic as laid down in Preamble to the Constitution of India. The term Indian, that is Bharatiya, thus signifies a citizen of the Republic of India, which bridges with Part II of the Constitution of India, under Articles 5 to 11, (i.e. defines the scope of Indian citizenship). To ideologically articulate the scope and nature of ancient Bharatiya Republic, re-interpreted in modern terms, and within the Constitutional framework, i.e. amplified by the harmony with its time tested ancient Hindu ethos is Ram Rajya that Mahatma Gandhi had propagated during the Freedom Struggle against British Imperialism.

Today's India is perceived by patriots as an ancient Hindu nation, a continuing Hindu civilization in search of a renaissance, based on modernization. Minorities need not have any fear of this representation of modern India in Hindu terms, since the Hindu heritage means respect for the minority as demonstrated in our history with Syrian Christians, Arab Muslim traders, Parsis, and Jews. Parsis who were brutally persecuted by invading Muslim hordes in their home country Persia, came to India for refuge, and Jews from Palestine subject to holocaust in the world by Muslims and Christians, lived in India in a safe sanctuary and protected. All these above-named minorities have pursued their goals of life in India without interference from the overwhelming majority Hindu community, and even today are protected by the Constitution of India.

MODERN HINDUTVA IMPERATIVES

Modernization is mind development that takes place because of the stock of current knowledge absorbed through education, new research, and also learning. This knowledge is expanded and pursued with character seeking to liberate and empower the human and not to enslave one. For this religious philosophy has helped to develop character necessary for imbibing knowledge in an enlightened way. India today leads the world in the supply pool of youth, i.e., persons in the age group of 15 to 35 years, and this lead will be concrete for another forty years. Also, this generation is most fertile milieu for promoting knowledge, innovation, and research. It is the prime work force that saves for the future, the corpus for pension funding of the old. We should therefore not squander this "natural vital resource." Modern economic growth also is powered overwhelming (over 65% of GDP) by new innovation and techniques (e.g., internet). More capital and labour contributes less than 35% of growth in GDP. Hence, we must by proper policy for the young, realize and harvest the demographic potential for material and spiritual advancement.

The four Varna (meaning color—white, saffron blue and green), or what in the West is termed as "caste system," was created to foster a special class, but is not birth based. To research and propagate this quality—a Varna (white) are called the Brahmins. Brahmins were venerated because they led a simple life, depending on donations of society, and were devoted education and religious theology. That is, being Gyani and Tyagi. Without these two rigorous attributes, one cannot be a Brahmin even if one is born of Brahmin parents. The "caste" system (i.e., Varna or Jati) was never meant to create a Brahmin hegemony or was conceived to be birth based. To become a rishi or a sage it was not necessary to be born of Brahmin parents. Valmiki, Veda Vyasa, Vishwamitra, and Kalidasa were not born in Brahmin families. Nor were Brahmins above the law. Ravana, a Brahmin scholar of repute had to pay a heavy price with his life for his abduction of the wife of Sri Rama, a Kshatriya. Varna identification instead was by gunas (virtues or qualities), as Lord Krishna told Arjuna according to the Gita. Krishna in the Bhagavad Gita says: '*caturvarnyam maya srishtam guna-karma vibhagashah*'. (Bhagavat Gita Chapter 4 Sloka 13) This means: *"The four classification (varna) are made by me based on character (guna) and duties (karma)."* In due course, this became perverted as 'caste' based on birth—today, which we hold as a serious corruption of our dharma and a pernicious illegitimate division of Hindu society. Additionally, the recent researches on DNA of Indians shows no racial differences amongst Varna or jati i.e., castes as propagated by British Imperialists and their brainwashed tutees in academia even today.

Thus, as a national policy we must treat the stock of young population irrespective of the ossified caste system as our potential demographic dividend. China is the second largest world leader in young population today, but the youth population in China has started shrinking from 2017, because of lagged effect of their ill-thought one-child policy. Japanese and European total populations have been aging fast, and will start declining in absolute numbers from following year. The US will however hold a steady trend thanks to a liberal policy of immigration, especially from Mexico and Philippines. But even then, the US will have a demographic shortage in skilled personnel in a decade. All currently developed countries thus experience a demographic deficit. But India will not. Our past alleged liability, by a fortuitous turn of fate, has now being globally regarded as our potential asset in the 21st century known as the "Knowledge Era." Thus, the primary objective of education was to prepare the mind in all its facets. This training of the mind and the process of thinking were considered as pre-requisites and essential for the acquisition of knowledge. Today, the West has re-invented this concept in the development of the intelligence in 7 (seven) dimensions-cognitive, emotional, social, moral, environmental, innovational and spiritual intelligences. Thus, now India has by unintended consequences been, gifted with a demographic dividend of young population. If we educate this youth to develop and attain a high quotient of *cognitive intelligence* (CQ) to become original thinkers, imbibe *emotional intelligence* (EQ) to have team spirit and rational risk-taking attitude, inculcate *moral intelligence* (MQ) to blend personal ambition with national goals, *cultivate social intelligence* (SoQ) to defend civic rights of the weak, gender equality and the courage to fight injustice, to protect environment, innovate new technologies, and nurture *spiritual intelligence* (SQ) to invoke the transformative power of vision meditation, and intention to access the vast energy the pervades the cosmos to do out of box research, then we can develop a superior species of human being, a modern Indian youth who can be relied on and be capable to contribute to make India a global power within two decades. Computers may have high CQ because they are programmed to understand the rules, and follow them without making mistakes. Many mammals have high EQ. Only humans know to ask why, and can work with re-shaping boundaries instead of just within boundaries. Humans unlike animals, can innovate. The human being is constituted by soul, mind and body and functions on its intelligence and power of discrimination (vivek). The main objective, in fact, of Sanatana Dharma is to unfold the tremendous multi-dimensional potentialities of human intelligence, step by step, from the outer physical body level to subtle inner mental to intellectual, and ultimately to the highest spiritual level, leading to Enlightenment and Self Realization. Thus, there is no conflict or contradiction between Hindutva and Modernization.

What needs to be discussed is how to inculcate Hindutva so that a modern mindset can be acquired? and how the modernization process can be structured so that Hindutva dimensions can be imbibed through our educational and family systems?

The value system that we seek to nurture today is on the basis of our ancient wisdom, to modernize and optimize our behavior for social and economic change, or in other words, to inculcate the quality of being a renaissance Hindustani, or possessing the attribute modernized Hindutva. Hindu value system is a balance between hard skills (such as learning arts and science) and soft skills (such as morals and spirituality).

Hindutva means that society adulates knowledge and places it in reverence above military power or wealth. Thus, society is structured with those who are Gyanis and Tyagis at the apex of the Social Order. We find these values conceptually elaborated by Lord Krishna in the Bhagavat Gita and the practice of it as propounded by Patanjali in his Yogasutras. But we cannot simply read the texts and learn these gems of wisdom, because these have to be re-interpreted in the modern context by our spiritual gurus of today. But three values (dharma) are core to a Hindu mindset or mental make-up:

Firstly, God in Sanatana Dharma does not favor anyone as other religions propagate. What you get is based on the Law of Karma. If you pray to God for rewards very sincerely then he may re-schedule your good karmas but not erase your bad karmas. It's bad consequences will be postponed to later life. Of course, unexhausted karmas carry over to next life. Prayers with deep sincerity also add to good Karma.

Secondly, a value prescribed in the Gita, i.e. one has complete freedom of action but that the fruits of those actions are determined by a calculus of accumulated past and present karmas, audited by God. (Gita 2:27)

Thirdly, the Varna social system has today degenerated into a birth-based oppressive cartelized system that requires to be repaired to bring it in consonance with its original meaning.

In its original pristine purity, Varna system was conceptualized as decentralization of power i.e. power of knowledge, weapons, wealth, and land respectively. The most important theme of Hindutva is the freedom of the spirit to inquire and the Law of Karma. Just as, science insists on freedom in exploring the physical world, Sanatana Dharma embodies freedom in the exploration of the spiritual realm. But to do this, requires mental and physical discipline, and the yamas and niyamas provide the code by which the freedom to attain spiritual enlightenment and bliss can be enjoyed.

Karma empowers one to do good and be satisfied with results of your effort whatever it may be. This is the mindset of Hindutva.Also, now, there is no reason to tolerate the present ossified practice of the "caste" system which at the very least, is obsolete and a stumbling block in the way of Hindu unity. Thus, we need to find a way to campaign for the abolition of the caste system so that we may achieve a renaissance in Hinduism and form a Virat Hindu polity. Re-building of the Grand Ram Temple in Ayodhya is the first step for that.

MODERN HINDUTVA MINDSET

We have already defined Hindustani as one who is a Hindu, or one who is not, but we need to acknowledge that his or her ancestors were Hindus. He or she need not be a citizen of India to be a Hindustani in contrast to the concept of Bharatiya. Hindu is the concept of our Asmita [identity]. The term Indian, that is Bharatiya, includes those living in India or living abroad as citizens of the Republic of India that is Bharat. India has been known as Bharat in the ancient Hindu religious texts, since time immemorial (e.g., Rig Veda at 3.52.12, the mantra of Maharishi Visvamitra), hence the implication is that modern India is a continuing entity and not a new Republic nation that was formed in 1950, and distinct from our ancient past.

Thus, India of today is the continuation of the past and is the outcome of Hindus ultimate victory, however imperfect and truncated, over foreign Islamic and Christian proselytizing aggressors. hence, Indians are people, who have always constituted a nation, living in a geographical location spanning from Kashmir to Kanyakumari bound together in a continuing civilization of more than 10,000 years. People who are mostly of Hindu religious faith and the remaining of those others of separate but equally respected faiths, whose ancestry scientifically determined in DNA and Genetic studies is however Hindu. The correct perception is that Indians are people who have always constituted a nation living in a geographical location spanning from Kashmir to Kanyakumari, from Cuttack to Car Nicobar, Diu to Dibrugarh, summarized in every Hindu prayer as "Asetu Himachalam," and bound together in a continuing unbroken civilization of much more than 10,000 years. This is how the word Indian has evolved. Arabs even today refer to Indians of all faiths as "Hind." Chinese from centuries have called us as "Yindu." China has always, and even now in all its Official publications, still refers to India by the name "Yindu Guo" which translated is "Hindu Rashtra." "Hindu" is described in the Constitution of India (Article 25, Explanation II) as one who is not a Muslim, Christian. This means that at present about 82.5% of the population of India are, according to the Constitution of India, Hindus including Buddhists, Jain, and Sikhs. Zoroastrians also should have also been counted as Hindus on the same basis, since in the Rig Veda, as a group described as Poru bear uncanny similarity to the Zoroastrians. The holy Gathas of the Zoroastrians are similar to the Vedas. The sage Sri Chandrashekhara Sarasvati, the Shankaracharya of Kanchi Kamakoti, has stated that Parsi Prophet Zarathustra was originally from Saurashtra. One version of the origin of the word "Hindu" is to trace it as the word derived from the sandhi of "Hi of Himalaya" and "Indu" of Indu Sagar.

The mindset created by the British imposed system was that Indians should be obedient to an oppressive foreign ruler and have a deep inferiority complex about the British. Thus, accept passively the status quo of those in power. That system too is more or less continuing today in a different context. This situation now urgently needs to change if our nation has to undergo a renaissance and achieve its potential. Our nation today has the world's largest number of young persons below the age of 25 years which is now known as our potential demographic dividend. If the nation is to reap this dividend then India's youth needs to mature into a dynamic, rational risk-taking, educated individuals with developed intelligence, and motivated to think out of the box to engage in research and develop essential innovations for national progress, and thus usher in the nation's rapid growth.

The youth also need to imbibe patriotism and spiritual values to put national interest above narrow personal and parochial interests and not consumed by greed and jealousy. In a nut shell, the youth must be educated to understand his or her national identity and destiny, and develop not just cognitive intelligence as at present, but several other dimensions of this human intelligence. Universities are green houses for our youth to find their roots and develop and flower their intelligence for pursuit of their chosen careers after graduation and to live a good family life in a vibrant democracy. Unfortunately, the educational system we have today is basically the same as designed by Macaulay in 1835, with intention to produce civil servants and clerks for the British to rule over the Indian masses. Since 1947 we have merely expanded that design to learn by rote the cognitive sciences without developing a questioning mind and curiosity to seek ways to innovate for a better future. A secure career without risk is the goal of every student even today. To understand his or her identity, the youth must know what their roots are. In particular, what is their affinity with other Bharatiyas and destiny of India. Thus, education must include tuition to make the youth aware of what is India and in which direction the nation must move. At present, India's youth learn nothing on how to anchor their values, except on unthinking adherence to the Western or European mores. Freedom Movement leaders such as Mahatma Gandhi, Sardar Patel, Netaji Subash Chandra Bose and Bharat Ratna Dr. Ambedkar had clearly wanted India after 1947 to develop, rooted in its ancient wisdom, language, and heritage. The call for Hindutva has been held by the Hon'ble Supreme Court in Manohar Joshi case [1996 SCC (1) 169] to be within the Constitutional requirements of free speech. Hence, time has arrived for us to openly declare India as an ancient Hindu civilization, which is the only way we can perform the Fundamental Duty under Article 51-A(f), and boldly up revere our sacred symbols. For example, the total ban on cow slaughter in Article 48 has been held by a 1958 Constitution Bench to possess constitutionality in the sense that the total ban is held to be a reasonable restriction on fundamental rights of all Indians.

In 1951, the Division Bench of the Madras High Court in the common judgment reported in 1952 I MLJ 557, the Bench construed the word 'denomination' (mentioned in Article 26 of the Constitution of India) while denoting to the Webster's dictionary. In the Appeal filed in the Hon'ble Supreme Court of India, also called the "Shirur Mutt Case" heard by Seven-Judge Constitutional Bench, definition of the word denomination was adopted from the westernized Oxford new English dictionary ignoring the facts of the religious and civilizational ethos of the Country. The concept of denomination is a western concept, where one denomination automatically excludes members of another denomination, from their religious institutions including places of worship, even if the other denomination belongs to its own religion. This is espoused from the concept of baptism to burial in Christian churches.

In the Hindu religion, members of one "sampradaya," do not exclude or deny opportunities to worship and participate to those who primarily follow other sampradayas or no sampradayas. Religious Sects were already portrayed as denominations by almost all English Dictionaries, old and modern. Adding preconditions of "common name, faith and organization" was not just superfluous but also incorrect since only non-Sects required such conditions. This incoherent definition continues to dilute fundamental constitutional rights of Hindu till date. While, seeking to know the precise connotation of the term "religious denomination" and from an Indic purview, Courts should consider the Hindi Version of the Constitution where equivalent term given for the word denomination is sampradaya. With respect to this regard one must refer to a decisive Article 394-A.

Furthermore, the definition as described in the famous Shirur Mutt case is out-lawed and outdated, because subsequently, the 42nd amendment to Constitution of India, was enacted during the Emergency in 1975 by the Indian National Congress government headed by Indira Gandhi and made India a "Socialist Secular" Republic. It is to be noted that, the said definition of a "religious denomination" is not read with the true essence of same and therefore, should be revised. Hon'ble Courts should ensure that they recognize sampradayas and their anubaghs as denominations and cloak them with the protection of Article 26 which confers on all religious denominations and sections thereof is the need of the hour.

That students of law are often taught that common law is precedent law and on the basis of which back in 1950's and 1960's judgements were passed in independent India. It is critical to analyze that the common law based on precedent during that era was of the Canon law or church law. As a result, the judicial system of our country derived principally from the British system. However, borrowing heavily either from the individual rights theory from the time of European renaissance, or following the English Common law, is nothing but another name for Church law. Monitored by which the Shirur Mutt Case was adjudicated leaving behind how India's idea of time, logic, and pranama differ with the west at a fundamental level, creating an unbridgeable distance between the administrated people and the judicial system.

There is a resilient demand and requisite for the society to get promising judicial review and pronouncements on getting Government Control out of Shrines and temples. The "common" law is nothing but part of English law that is derived from custom and judicial precedent rather than statutes. Now, English customs being reflected in Indian judicial pronouncements via out-lawed or inconsistent interpretation of definitions of religious denomination will go against the very essence of the Constitution of India and cultural ethos protected by the same supremacy of law enacted.

Though, Indian culture was always a Bottom-Up Approach culture. Framers of the Constitution played a fundamental role behind it as they decided to impose their version upon, without their being much consultation or discussion with people on the ground. Now, it resulted in a Top-Down Approach, in terms of the value of the Constitution upholds while referring to the socialistic characteristic embraced in its habitat where the state is given precedence over other entities within the Indian

Republic. There would had there been an organic set-up, would have been a bottom-up approach; certain approach or idea of the Constitution would have been different including certain matters of religion. The idea of Secularism was also connoted with a top-down approach, if you went with a bottom-up approach, as we can see now it is the grass-root that required a religious driven identity in the Indian polity. Still the Constitution encirclements certain rudiments which helps in getting that right-minded identity. Under the directive principles of State policy, framers crafted certain norms for good governance like the Uniform Civil Code and abolishing on cow slaughters which is also observed as held by the Apex Judicial body of the Country. Courts should dictate a more organic approach with respect to Temples being under the control of Government and utilization of funds with respect to its activities. Through the epoch of 1839 to 1842 in India, a very westernized approach over temples was comprehensively imposed. Correspondingly, on the notion of Christian management of temples government in India, Judiciary of Britain wrote a missive to the then Government general of British government in India, to withdraw their clouts to administer and superintend the Hindu Temple and to hand-over the same to the concerned forerunner with faith in Hindu religion. Furthermore, during this period the revenue collected from shrines, trusts and temples were all consigned with the British Government in India. Indirectly the income of charitable Trusts and temples were appropriated by the British government which reflects that they did not had faith on local trustees. The income spawned, was spent for Non-Hindu purposes under the grab of social causes and for their own imposition of ideology in Indians. On actual, the government did not handover the sway to the local trustees and local heads of Mutts and temples. If we track the era before colonization took place in India, the damage altogether started with Mughal rule, how throughout the Mughal or the Islamic subjugation, the destruction of ancient, divine and holiest Hindu temples took place.

At present the Government has been taking over Hindu temples, its resources and land and has been using it for all kinds of non-religious purposes under the states enacted Hindu Religious Institutions and Charitable Endowment Acts on the pretext of maladministration of the temple properties. Under Article 31A of the Constitution of India such a take-over cannot be permanent. If mal-administration charge is true, then the Government should rectify it within a reasonable period such as three years, and then hand it back. At present State governments have taken over tens of thousands of temples for decades. Now is the time to get them released.

In India before 1757, centers of dance, art or culture or now referred to as Temples were governed by the local communities to benefit the community in the form of institutions for education called "pathshalas," Cow-shelters or "gau-shalas," or feed the poor. Temples were an establishment to perform important economic, social, artistic and cerebral functions in ancient and medieval India. Serving as nuclei of the aforementioned, temples also managed local elaboration task of many relief projects or assisting with agricultural developments. To support such eloquent role in the growth and nurturement of the society, devotees, Kings, Queens, merchants and other officials in the kingdom(s) contributed to the Hundi because they understood the prominence and importance of such place and its significant position in the society. The same can be corroborated as the faith of people was enshrined in the society with an attitude of a certain way of life. Temples also served as boat for the needy to sail as they provided them with employment and social opportunities to have an organic and a virtuous standard of living. It was also, seen how temples vested with such large gold and silver coins from grants of royal patrons, became a hub for banking while providing infrastructural improvement to the society. Temples became establishments and patrons of economic commotion. Being a heart of social network in the society and community growth, temples could play a key role in our country and shape our nation's economic, socio and political scenario in a healthier way if the westernized or the "organized Revenue-system" of the British did not encumbered or impeded in the society. Temples being the heart for learning, contributed towards the education of children through schools called "mathas," an epicenter where "Vedas" were embedded in learning process. While also, functioned as a setting for "parikshas" (tests), vad-vivad(s) (debates) or team contests and Vedic recitals. When British came, they focused primarily on two things, the structured or a well-codified criminal legal mechanism or to generate higher taxes and revenue. With respect to the criminal system, they codified the Indian Penal Code, 1860 or the Evidence Act, 1872, to have a centralized and common Criminal Law. They never focused on the Uniformity in the Civil Code. To generate high revenue and taxes they concentrated on capitalizing of the core abode of the society i.e. shrines or temples. The devotion shown by devotees and Hindu rulers during the Vijayanagar Empire which was a high historical point, replacing as a champion culture against the aggressions of other Mughal or Islamic rule was all under the control of British Raj. They introduced various forms of organized system to seize control over and have dominion over the vast wealth of the temples. Under the British Raj, supplemented by the needs of the colonial power, the education system of India was also developed to suit the purpose of hegemony on the mind-sets of the future generations. The colonial interests of the British always shaped the then educational policies of India making them all westernized and white washing the cultural ethos of the society.

Knowing the value and stature of temples in India, British had a pre-determined stratagem to breakdown the system of Temples in India to banquet and triumph with respect to the schema of colonization. So, they decided to introduce the Madras Regulation VII of 1817. Although in 1840, Christian missionaries did not like the idea of Christians managing Hindu temples and decided to return the temples to their trustees. This document named House of Commons Papers, is a document containing communications from the particular individuals connected with different temples and the officials at Fort Saint George. It says that when Idolatry Act was made compulsory in England, the Church officials barred all British officials in India to stay away from direct management of all the temples, they were used to manage before. As such the British tried to give away the management of all the temples, to an undisputed local body who will in return report to them and submit all revenue. In this process, Regarding Tirumala temple, they found Mahant of Hathiramjee Mutt, suitable for managing entire administration of the Tirumala Hill temple. So, they decided to appoint Mahant as the Administrator of Tirumala temple from June 1843 onwards. When they took this decision, the other temple servants like the Pedda Jeeyangar Swami and other temple servants objected this appointment and claimed they are the right persons to be given the management of the temple. As such they wrote letters/petitions to Fort Saint George officials to claim the management. In these petitions, the

Thenkalai Sect people—Pedda Jeeyangar, themselves admitted that their entry into Tirumala Hill Shrine began only with Saint Ramanujacharya of 11th century and that their office continued for 900 years from then.

By 1858 the temple management was slowly handed over to trustees and in case of prominent temples, The Board of Revenue administered the management of large temples and did not want to lose hold of the same. Unpredictably, the introduction of the Religious Endowments Act 1863 was to hand over temple-running to the trustees from the British government. Till 1925, the administration was going smooth, but the introduction of the Madras Religious and Charitable Endowments Act 1925 came in. At that time, it included Muslims and Christians in it. Subsequently, wise-spread unrest was seen from Muslims and Christians against the Act. After two years, the Madras Hindu Religious and Endowments Act 1927 was implemented and was made applicable only to the Hindus. The British had differentiated and bifurcated in laws with respect to religion for Hindus and the rest. Critically mentioning that in 1925, the Sikh Gurdwaras Act was also passed which brought gurdwaras under the control of an elected body of Sikhs exclusively.

Now, we see that still numerous temples are under Government Control depriving of one's Right to administer and manage its own affairs in matters of religion and also to establish and maintain institutions for religious and charitable purposes. Also, with respect to management of the temple by government, the management cannot be for time immemorial, the same can be for a limited period that too in Public Interest or proper management. Taking over of the management of any property by the State can only be for a limited period as per the Supreme Law or the Constitution of India. The Hon'ble Supreme Court in this case of State eternal annexation of the Sri Sabanayagar Temple [(2014) V SCC 75] in the town of Chidambaram held in para 65 that even if the management of a temple is taken over to remedy an evil, the management must be handed over to the person concerned immediately after the evil stands remedied. Continuation thereafter would tantamount to usurpation of their proprietary rights or violation of the fundamental rights guaranteed by the Constitution in favor of the persons deprived. Building upon this, the authors' have also co-petitioned a Writ Petition in the Hon'ble High Court of Andhra Pradesh to further liberate Sri Venkateswaraswamy Temple at Tirumala and Sri Padmavathy Temple in Tiruchaanur and another 11 temples part of the schedule of the Andhra Pradesh Charitable and Hindu Religious Institutions and Endowments Act, 1987 and under the TTD Board (government administered board) in Andhra Pradesh from State government control.

These constitutionally valid pillars are what Hindutva is, and it is significant that Hindutva goals can be achieved within the present Constitution. Throughout ancient Indian history, Hindu kingdoms, never required any 'subject' to be of Hindu religion in order to be regarded a first-class citizen. Only in Asoka's reign and Islamic rule, India was a theocracy. A Hindu is naturally 'Secular'. But secularism is a much-bandied-about subject nowadays. Unfortunately, those political parties who have been swearing by it all these years have failed to persuade the masses that secularism is good for the country. In fact, secularism as defined and propagated today has lost its relevance. The concept as understood by the masses of India stands thoroughly discredited. Hence the question is whether we should redefine secularism in keeping our civilization tradition to make it acceptable to the masses or capitulate to the rising fundamentalism in the country with dire consequences for national integrity and security. When Remarking Luther had defined secularism in Europe, it simply meant that the power of the state would be exercised independently from the directions of the Church. Thus, a secular government would act to safeguard the nation-state, even if such action was without Church sanction. Later, Marx calling religion the 'opium of the masses' defined secularism to completely eschew religion.

In India, Jawaharlal Nehru and his followers subscribed to the later Marxist redefinition of the concept in which even in public functions, cultural symbolism such as lighting a lamp to inaugurate a conference or breaking a coconut to launch a project was regarded as against secularism. This orthodoxy induced a reaction in the Indian masses. Nehru failed to define what historical roots ought to be a part of the Modern Indian, and what was to be rejected. In the name of 'scientific temper', he rejected most of our past as 'obscurantism'. His orthodox secularism sought to alienate the Indian from his hoary past. Since nearly 85 percent of Indians are pan-Hindu in beliefs, and Hindu religion from its inception has been without a 'Church', 'Pope' or 'Book' (in contra-distinction to Christianity), therefore neither Martin Luther nor Marx made any sense to the Indian masses. Since there was little political challenge to Nehru after the untimely death of Gandhiji and Patel, the Marxian secularism concept superficially prevailed till Nehru's demise in 1964. The masses therefore humored Nehru without accepting his concept of secularism. A Conceptual void however remained to be filled. But Congress Party continued thereafter to fail to provide a political concept of secularism by which an Indian citizen could comprehend how he should bond "secularly" with another citizen of a different religion or language, or region and feel equally Indian. The Hindu instinctively could not accept the idea that India was what the British had put together, and that the country was just an area incorporated by the imperialists. Such a ridiculous idea, fostered quixotically by Jawaharlal Nehru University historians, found just no takers amongst the Indian people. Thus, the void remained, but the yearning in the masses to be "Indian" grew over the years with growth of mass media. Therefore, this void had to be filled and the yearning of national identity required to be articulated for the masses. The legal perspective on Indian secularism has been brilliantly analyzed by the Hon'ble Supreme Court Justice Aftab Alam in 2009. While he disapproves of the trends in, and import of, the various Supreme Court decisions since 1994 as creeping Hindutva, We, however welcome his critical analysis. But we salute his research, which we have used in this Chapter in fact to prove our point viz., the Indian Constitution, as increasingly interpreted by the Hon'ble Supreme Court, is basically becoming 'Hindutva-friendly'. It has to be because of the founding fathers of our Republic in the Constituent Assembly left no doubt that the Constitution was to be Hindutva friendly. What Jawaharlal Nehru preached Congress Party's secularism was alien to our Vedic legacy the Constitution of India recognizes twenty-two languages as Indian languages. Indians speaking the same language may belong to different religions. India is home to eight major religions of the world. Conversely, Indians belonging to the same religious group may come from different parts of the national geography and may speak different languages, dress differently, eat different kinds of food in entirely different manners and may have completely different social and economic concerns.

In India, religion, a democratic State and secularism overlap and combine to display a highly interesting and unique society.

India has survived while others with the same concerns have balkanized. But the important fact is that the liberality implicit in the Indian system is owed to the Hindu ethos of our civilization. The Indian Constitution does not have any provision, unlike the First Amendment of the United States Constitution, proscribing the making of any law respecting an establishment of religion. It instead recognizes religion as a source of law. With a view to protect minority rights, it confers affirmative social and cultural rights on religious groups. It guarantees the fundamental freedom of religion but enables the State, to regulate religious practices on certain limited grounds of morality, health and public order.

Thus, under the Indian Constitution, secularism of the State involves a plural establishment of religion with the State but maintaining of equidistance from all religions. The Court is called upon, in a variety of ways, to oversee and regulate the distance that the State ought to keep from religious establishments and the nature of State intervention permissible in religious affairs. In that sense it would be more appropriate to designate India as a spiritual state rather than a secular state. But confusion prevails today in the judiciary on how far to stretch secularism and how cognizant the law should be of the Hindu ethos of the nation. For instance, keeping a beard by a Muslim student is invoked Article 25 of the Constitution that gives to every person (in this case the Muslim student) the freedom of conscience and free profession and practice of religion. A Christian missionary-run school defends its rules i.e. not to permit students with beards and expelled the Muslim student on the basis of Article 30[1] of the Constitution of India

[1]Article 30. Right of minorities to establish and administer educational institutions.

that gives to all minorities (in this case the Christian) the right to establish and administer educational institutions. The expulsion was challenged unsuccessfully before the Hon'ble High Court and the matter finally came to the Hon'ble Supreme Court. On 30-3-2009 the petition was dismissed in limine (at the threshold) but in course of the brief hearing, one of the judges made certain observations that were widely reported in the media. The Judge had said: "We don't want to have Talibans in the country. Tomorrow a girl student may come and say that she wants to wear a burqa, can we allow it?"[2] He further said: "We should strike a balance between rights and personal beliefs. We cannot overstretch secularism." In furtherance, the Hon'ble Judge added: "You can join some other institution if you do not want to observe the rules. But you can't ask the school to change the rules for you."

The remarks created an uproar among the Muslims against the remarks calling the beard and the burqa as a mark of the Taliban. Then, on 06-07-2009, on a review petition, the same Bench recalled its order dismissing the petition and requested the Hon'ble Chief Justice to have the case placed before some other Bench. On 11-09-2009 the case came up before another

(1) All minorities, whether based on religion or language, shall have the right to establish and administer educational institutions of their choice.

(1A) In making any law providing for the compulsory acquisition of any property of an educational institution established and administered by a minority, referred to in clause (1), the State shall ensure that the amount fixed by or determined under such law for the acquisition of such property is such as would not restrict or abrogate the right guaranteed under that clause.

(2) The state shall not, in granting aid to educational institutions, discriminate against any educational institution on the ground that it is under the management of a minority, whether based on religion or language.

[2](Times of India, March 31, 2009). (*Source*)

Bench. And this time the response of the Court was completely different: "How on earth could a school disentitle a student from pursuing studies just because he has kept a beard? Then there will be no end to such prima facie ridiculous rules." This exemplifies the difficulties faced by the Court in dealing with two 'competing' constitutional rights in Articles 25 and 30. The first Bench obviously gave precedence to the group right guaranteed by the Constitution (Article 30) to a religious minority, in this case the Christian management of the school. The second Bench, on the other hand, deemed fit, in the context of the case, to uphold the right of the individual (Article 25), the Muslim boy. This deep dilemma, as Hon'ble Justice Alam pointed out, seems to run through the decisions of the Hon'ble Supreme Court on the issue of cultural and educational rights guaranteed by the Constitution of India to the religious minorities.

In 1957, the Communist Government of Kerala enacted a law, bringing the school education under the State's extensive control. A number of Christian organizations and some Muslim groups threatened to create a political crisis. The Hon'ble President of India to whom the Bill had come for his assent therefore made a reference to the Hon'ble Supreme Court on the constitutional validity of the Bill. A Constitution Bench of seven Judges, headed by Chief Justice S.R. Das, heard the matter (AIR 1958 SC 956) and held that Article 30 was a stand-alone Article and the right guaranteed to the minorities under it was not controlled either by Article 29 or any other Article in the chapter of fundamental rights, or even Article 45 in the chapter of Directive Principles relating to education to children below the age of six years. Speaking for the Court S.R. Das, Chief Justice . said: "... So long as the Constitution stands as it is and is not altered, it is, we conceive, the duty of this Court to uphold the fundamental rights and thereby honor our sacred obligation to the minority communities who are our own" (p.986). The decision in Kerala Education Bill, 1957, however, was not unanimous. There was at least one dissenting voice (of Justice T.L.Venkatarama Aiyar.). He took the view that Article 30 was primarily intended to protect educational institutions established for the conservation and promotion of the culture, language or religion of a minority group and thus created a purely negative obligation on the State and prevented it from interfering with minorities living in their own cultural life as regards religion or language. Justice Aiyar observed:

" ... Now, to compel the State to recognise those institutions would conflict with the fundamental concept on which the Constitution is framed that the State should be secular in character."(p.989)

The two views directly opposing each other and both relying upon the principles of secularism that were manifested in Kerala Education Bill appear to run through the decisions of the Hon'ble Supreme Court on all aspects of secularism. But with the sole exception in S. Azeez Basha v. Union of India (Aligarh Muslim University case (AIR 1968 SC 662)) the majority decision in Kerala Education Bill was relied upon to expand the scope of the right under Article 30, and five years later in Sidhrajbhai Sabbai v. State of Gujarat (AIR 1963 SC 540) a six-Judge Constitutional Bench went on to hold:

"The right (under) Article 30(1) is a fundamental right declared in terms absolute. Unlike the fundamental freedoms guaranteed by Article 19 it is not subject to reasonable restrictions."(p.547).

Soon secularism came to be regarded as not only a fundamental right but a part of the basic structure of the Constitution. In S. R. Bommai v. Union of India (the Bommai case) [(1994)3 SCC 1] seven out of the nine Judges constituting the Bench reiterated the view that secularism was the basic feature of the Constitution and in a case where State Government acted contrary to the constitutional mandate of secularism or, directly or indirectly, subverted the secular principles, that would tantamount to failure of the constitutional machinery and the State Government would make itself liable to dismissal under Article 356 (para 434).

But soon enough, the Court started to see the interplay between the community-based rights and individual rights in a new light. In St. Stephen's College, a Delhi Christian minority college the Court felt the need to strike a balance between an individual's right based on merits and the right of minorities to set up and administer educational institutions of their choice and directed that St. Stephen's College could have no more than fifty per cent seats reserved for Christian students. Thus, the right under Article 30 was for the first-time subject to Article 29 reversing the earlier ominous trend, for the better. Article 29 states: Protection of interests of minorities.—(1) Any section of the citizens residing in the territory of India or any part thereof having a distinct language, script or culture of its own shall have the right to conserve the same.

In 2005, this reversing trend was fortified by several decisions till in the end of Article 30 but all lost its independent identity. The position that emerges from these decisions may be summarized thus:

- The right to set up educational institutions and impart any kind of education at any level is available to every Indian citizen under Article 19(1)(g) of the Constitution as the right "to carry on any occupation, trade or business."
- Article 30 does not give to the religious minorities any additional or separate right. The religious minority has no special right that the majority does not have under the Constitution.

- Articles 29 and 30 do not confer any rights but afford certain protections to the minorities. The two articles can be better understood as a protection and/or a privilege of the minority rather than an abstract right. (View of Venkatarama, J. in minority of 1:6 in Kerala Education Bill, was thus resurrected)
- The right under Article 30 is not absolute. It is subject to Article 29(2) and other laws. It can be restricted in public interest and national interest.

The Hon'ble Supreme Court's perception of secularism, also underwent change since the Bommai case of 1994 through a catena of judgments since 1995. In 2002, a public interest litigation [(2002) 7 SCC368] was filed questioning the curriculum for school education framed by the National Council for Educational Research and Training on the ground that it was heavily loaded with religion and the contents of the Vedas. It was contended that the inclusion of religion, Sanskrit, Vedic Mathematics, Vedic Astrology, etc. in the courses of study for the schools was contrary to secular principles. Justice Dharmadhikari one of the members of the three-Judge Bench wrote a separate, though concurring judgment in which he discussed in some detail about the true nature of secularism. He observed that the doctrine of the State neutrality towards all religions was a narrow concept of secularism. He further observed that the policy of complete neutrality towards and apathy for all kinds of religious teachings in institutions of the State had not done any good to the country. The real meaning of secularism is 'sarva dharma samabhav' meaning *equal treatment and respect for all religions,* but, we have misunderstood the meaning of secularism as negation of all religions." (page 406-407)

In 2005, an organization representing a section of the Jain community came to the Court seeking a direction to the Central Government to notify "Jains" as a minority community. The Court not only firmly rejected the prayer but also expressed its strong disapproval of the very concept of "minority." Calling it a baggage from India's history, the Court noted (Bal Patil case, SCC p. 701, para 25): "Muslims constituted the largest religious minority because the Mughal period of rule was the longest followed by the British Rule during which many Indians had adopted Muslim and Christian religions."

It further observed that the concept of "minorities" was the result of the British policy of divide and rule that first led to the formation of separate electorates and reservations of seats on the basis of population of Hindus and Muslims and finally led to the partition of India and formation of a separate Muslim State of Pakistan. The Court pointed out that India was a democratic republic which had adopted the right to equality as its fundamental creed and hence, the constitutional ideal should be the elimination of "minority" and "majority" and the so-called forward and backward classes. All that remains now is further decisions of the Hon'ble Supreme Court to restrict the meaning of minorities to cover only ethnic minorities whose DNA is different from majority of Indians. That would mean only a few tribes of extreme Northeast and Onge tribes in Andaman's, but not Muslims and Christians who are not recent converts. However, Affirmative action of the State can be extended only to those minorities which have suffered from imposed social disabilities, and not those minorities which have been ruling classes.

The term 'Secularism' should also be replaced in the Constitution by the alternative more appropriate phrase: "spiritual state," based on 'Sarva Pantha Sama Bhava'. The majority-minority question has dogged India for the last seven decades and more years since Independence. Paradoxically, the Hindus despite being over 80% appear to suffer from a minority complex, because Hindus of today are being confused by others on whether the Republic of India founded in 1947 is a legatee of the ancient Hindu India, or a new nation altogether, forged as a by-product of British rule from a motley crowd of castes, ethnicities, and linguistic groups. This confusion is also at the core of the identity crisis which can ultimately be disappeared, only if we decide which one of two we constitute of or are: a continuing Hindu civilizational entity or an administrative by-product of British Imperialism. Minorities would in turn need to understand how to adjust with the Hindu majority and to its own sub-legacy of forced or induced conversions to Islam and Christianity by foreign invaders, and thus whereby this identity crisis is resolved. The present dysfunctional perceptional mismatch in the understanding of who are we as a people, is behind most of the communal tensions and inter-community distrust in the country. It also further weakens India's integrity. Unless Indians settle this question arising from these two conflicting concepts of identity clearly, finally, unambiguously, and authoritatively as to who we Indians are, Indians will flounder, flip-flop, and generally continue to be devoid of healthy patriotism. That is, we are Hindustanis of the soil of Bharat Mata.

CHAPTER 2

Ram Temple in Janmasthan for Renaissance

THE REASONS WHY/POINT OF DISPUTE

The Sri Ram Janma Bhoomi/Ayodhya dispute is not any ordinary temple-mosque dispute. It is not just any other temple. It is the Temple of Nativity of Bhagwan Sri Ramlala. The struggle of the Hindu society was to reclaim and regain the holy native Land/Birthplace of Bhagwan, and this Native Land in itself is a Deity and there can be no splitting up or division of the Deity.

Ramlala Virajman—is a perpetual minor and a juridical person—a legal entity—having a distinct identity and legal rights and obligations under the law. No other can have ownership rights over Bhagwan's property. The entire disputed land measures maximum about 1500 square yards (1500 X 9 = 13,500 square feet). The 67.4 acres of land acquired by the Government of India is separate from this over which there is no lawsuit pending in any Court. The entire site under consideration in the Court is that of Ramlala Virajman (Infant Sri Ram sitting at his Birthplace). It is the Place of Birth, Place of Pastimes, playing field and recreational area of Bhagwan. Describing the significance of this place, the Skanda Purana, written thousands of years ago, says that the Darshan (discerning/sighting/glimpse) of the holy birthplace of Sri Ram is liberating. The places of worship of adorable figures of any community can be constructed at many places, statues of great men can be put up at many places, but the places of manifestation/birth of great men/Deities would be at one place, and that can never be changed. The birthplace cannot be displaced, cannot be relocated. It is non-exchangeable. It cannot be swapped, bartered, sold or donated. As mentioned above, Ayodhya is to Hindus what Mecca is to Muslims. So, no new structure, establishment, institution, Centre, that that could take Hindus back to the outrageous memories of history must be built in Ayodhya. Fundamentally, the Constitution of India identifies the Author(s) right to pray at the exact same spot, along with every Hindu in the world. The fundamental Right to pray is enshrined under Article 25 of the Constitution of India and the liberty to faith, belief and worship is enshrined in the Preamble. Moreover, which is superior to an ordinary legal right to property as claimed by Muslims. The stature of Fundamental right as elucidated is superior to that of ordinary legal right to property.

History of Conflicts and Movements of Cases on Sri Ram Janma Bhoomi

The struggle to get back the birthplace continues unabated since 1528 CE (since the day invader Babur ordered demolition of the temple and superimposition of the triple-domed Jihadi statement/structure over it). The entire Hindu society has incessantly been waging this fight. The saint fraternity of Ayodhya and the kings/emperors of the areas around have had special contributions in this fight back. The pages of history record details of 76 battles for this cause. The history of battles speaks volumes about the fact that Hindus never ever gave up their claim over this place. These battles and struggles show that the occupation of this place by the Muslim invader and his descendants was never peaceful, continuous, uninterrupted.

In 1885 CE, an application was moved before the then government official on behalf of Nirmohi Akhara with a request to permit replacement of the thatched canopy by a concrete one above the Ramchabutra (raised-platform) located in the outer courtyard of the birthplace complex. On this subject, the British Judge Colonel FEA Chamier (Faizabad District Judge) declined permission, but in his verdict admitted that "... It is most unfortunate that a masjid should have been built on the land specially held sacred by the Hindus..."

At the Hindu Conference held at Muzaffarnagar in Uttar Pradesh in March 1983, the late Dau Dayal Khanna, a former Congress minister and U.P. State legislator, called upon the Ram devotees to "liberate the places of Ayodhya, Mathura and Kashi and bring back the glory of Hindustan." On April 07 and 08, 1984, a conference of saints took place at Vigyan Bhawan, New Delhi (First Dharma Sansad/Dharma Parliament). The Dharma Sansad prescribed and mandated the liberation of the Sri Ram Janma Bhumi at Ayodhya. Thus, with the directive of the Sant Fraternity, the Vishva Hindu Parishad started the 77th edition of the five centuries old struggle. The new struggle and pan-India movement was initiated by a public awareness campaign to open the locks put on the birthplace. The Ram-Janaki chariot was consecrated at Sitamarhi. On 7 October 1984, the Ram-Janaki Rath arrived at the banks of the Holy Saryu River in Ayodhya. Thousands of Ram devotees took Saryu Maharani's sacred waters in hand and vowed to liberate the Sri Ram Janma Bhumi. From October, 1985, public awareness campaign started again in Uttar Pradesh by 6 chariots under the banner of Ram Janma Bhumi Mukti Rath

Yatra. As a result, the locks put on the Sri Ram's Birthplace in the year 1949 CE were opened on 1 February 1986 by order of the court. There were several attempts made to stop public worship and prayers to Ramlala, but the court did not accept it.

After this, a series of public awareness campaigns started. The Ram Shila Pujan (consecration of clay, stone or marble bricks) programmes were organized in about 300,000 villages across the country. Consecrated bricks from across the country and abroad reached Ayodhya. In the presence of the revered saints and sages, the first foundation stone was laid for the grand Ram temple as per Hindu aspirations by Shri Kameshwar Chowpal, some Karyakarta/worker from amongst the Scheduled Castes brethren. This event was a wonderful example of the united strength of the Ram devotees as well as that of social harmony. Many programs like Ram Jyoti, Ramcharan Paduka Pujan, Vijay Mantra Jaap Abhiyan led to a unique awakening in the country.

On 24 June 1990, in Haridwar, in a meeting of the Kendriya Margdarshak Mandal it was decided to go to Ayodhya to perform Karseva on October 30, 1990 (Devotthan Ekadashi). The then Chief Minister of Uttar Pradesh made tricky cordon off plans around Ayodhya to plug up all entry points whatsoever to make Ayodhya out of bounds for all incoming devotees and declared that 'Not even a bird/avian can dare flap its wings here'. The Hindu society accepted this challenge and thousands of people managed to brave or tiptoe and/or creep into the town of Ayodhya from all directions despite all kinds of repression from police. The Karsevaks (volunteers) hoisted the saffron flags on the domes at the appointed time. Police firings martyred karsevaks. The firing incident of 2 November 1990 is known by all. At the end of the day, the government bowed down and all the karsevaks got permission to have darshan, and only then they returned home.Ten days of Satyagraha took place; thousands of people came every day. The ashes of the martyred Karsevaks were taken around the country and millions of people paid their homage to it.

On 4 April 1991, the historic *Virat Hindu Sammelan* was held at the Boat Club, New Delhi and an estimated 25 lakh (2½ million) Rama devotees attended this meeting. Even as the meeting was to conclude, the Chief Minister of Uttar Pradesh, Mulayam Singh Yadav resigned. There were re-elections in Uttar Pradesh, and subsequently, Sri Kalyan Singh became the Chief Minister. It was announced again that the Karseva would take place on 6 December 1992. Sri Kalyan Singh Ji announced that bullets won't be fired. Security forces were stationed around Ayodhya. The pent-up feelings of the society burst out due to the atrocities on the Ram devotees and fortuitously the Babri structure got deconstructed. Millions of Ram devotees participated in this phase of the Ram Janma Bhumi struggle started from 1984 CE. The resolve of the Ram devotees became stronger with every campaign.

At the midnight of 22-23 December 1949, there was manifestation of the Lord at Sri Ram Janma Bhumi. The administration locked the doors of the structure in the name of law & order. When the society objected, the court ordered the worship rituals of the Lord to be conducted every morning and evening by opening the locks and then the rituals continued daily. Even today, Ramlala is seated at the same place and worship is being done continuously. In January 1950, Gopal Singh Visharad, a resident of Gonda, filed his suit in the court praying that: "I am a devotee of the Lord! I come for daily darshan, so no person or the administration should put any hindrance in my darshan-poojan." The administration appointed a receiver to manage the place. In the year 1959, Nirmohi Akhada filed its suit in Faizabad Court praying that the government-appointed receiver be removed and the management handed over to it. On 18 December 1961, the Uttar Pradesh Sunni Muslim Waqf Board filed its case demanding that the triple-domed structure be declared a public mosque, and the worship paraphernalia inside the structure be removed. In July 1989, a case was filed on behalf of Bhagwan Ramlala Virajman and the Native Land Janma Bhumi making them party to the case; the Lord Himself presented His side. In 1989, the above four suits were transferred from the lower court to the Lucknow Bench of Allahabad High Court for a collective hearing. The government was too late in appreciating the feelings of the public. As a result, the pent-up feelings of the society burst out on 6 December 1992. Everyone knows the result. After the deconstruction of the structure, the so-called disputed land, and the 67 acres of land of Hindu society spread around it, was acquired by the Government of India by a law (Act 33/1993) on 07th January, 1993.

Against the said takeover, a Muslim gentleman named Ismail Faruqi went to the Supreme Court in 1993 and demanded that the mosque site could not be acquired. On 7 January 1993, the then President of India referred a question to the Supreme Court of India under Article 143 of the Constitution for consideration and opinion thereon. The question was: *"WHETHER A HINDU TEMPLE OR ANY HINDU RELIGIOUS STRUCTURE EXISTED PRIOR TO THE CONSTRUCTION OF THE RAM JANAM BHUMI-BABRI MASJID (INCLUDING THE PREMISES OF THE INNER AND OUTER COURTYARDS OF SUCH*

STRUCTURE) IN THE AREA ON WHICH THE STRUCTURE STOOD?" (vide 1994 (6) SCC p. 360 Ismail Faruqi vs. Union of India).A constitution bench of five judges was set up in the Supreme Court to find an answer to the petition challenging the takeover and the President's question. After about 22 months of hearing, the Constitution Bench returned the President's question respectfully, without answering it, and wrote that the situation obtaining at the site prior to 1528 CE could be answered only on the basis of science and archaeology. At the same time, the Supreme Court, by a majority verdict, cancelled the acquisition of the disputed land and ordered the resumption of all the cases related to the disputed land. It also said that the Government of India would maintain the status quo of the disputed land and would protect it. The Supreme Court accepted the acquisition of the entire 67 acres of land by the Government of India except the disputed land.

This lawsuit is known as Dr. M. Ismail Faruqui Etc, Mohd. ... vs Union of India And Others, which was decided in October 1994. In 1995 CE, in the Lucknow Bench of Allahabad High Court, a bench of three judges was constituted and it heard for 15 years all the suits related to Sri Ram Janma Bhumi in the manner of a trial court. To know the situation of the site prior to 1528 CE, the Hon'ble Full Bench of Lucknow High Court, had ordered Geo-Radiological Survey (Ground Penetrating Radar Survey) by Canadian experts on 01.8.2002 and then to verify the truth of the GPRS report, the HC had ordered for excavation around the site by the Archaeological Survey of India (ASI of GOI) on 23.10.2002.The Lucknow Bench of Allahabad High Court, on the basis of the GPRS Report and the ASI's excavation report, made it clear in its the 30th September,

2010 verdict that prior to 1528 CE a Hindu temple was in existence at the disputed site. The High Court, while outrightly dismissing the suits of the Nirmohi Akhara and the Sunni Waqf Board, wrote that no relief could be given to them. On the contrary, it accepted the suit of Ramlala Virajman, but ordered a three-way partition and equal distribution of the disputed land among the three parties which was not justifiable.

Due to this unjudicious move, it became necessary to move an appeal in the Supreme Court. All appeals were filed in December 2010. Till July 2017, the turn of the appeals to be heard did not come. When the Hon'ble Supreme Court saw the case for the first time in August 2017, it was found that the documents in Hindi, Sanskrit, Persian, Urdu and French languages needed to be translated into English. The Uttar Pradesh government got about 14,000 pages translated into English in 4 months. During the hearing of the appeal in the Hon'ble Supreme Court on 29 October 2018, the court remarked that this appeal was not in their priority, and so the trial got deferred till January 2019. At the same time, the court ordered that the trial would be heard by a five-judge bench.

NARRATION OF THE CONFLICT(S) (inclusive of 2018 Judgment [AIR 2018 SC 5134])

The ultimate myth is that the issue tracks down just to the 90's. it is incorrect and factually, historically wrong to say that. The matter locates down to 1528 when the Babri Mosuqe was built in Ayodhya on the land of Ram-Janmabhoomi (birth place of the God-King Rama). Mir Baqi, one of the Mughal King Babur's Generals', destroyed a pre-existing temple of Lord Ram and built Babri Masid at the holy site. After that, in 1859 the British presidency instituted a screen to separate the place of worship, consenting the inner-court to be used by the Muslims and outer-court by the Hindus. In 1885, a suit was filed in the Court of the Sub-Judge, Faizabad against the Secretary of State for India. The suit was filed to seek permission to construct a temple on the Ram-Chabutra (adjoining the Babri configuration). To which, in 1886, District Judge of Faizabad Court FEA Chamber [an Englishman] dismissed the permission and Suit saying "it is most unfortunate that a masjid should have been built on land specially held scared by the Hindus, but as that event occurred 356 years ago, it is too late now to remedy the grievance." It can be very well inferred that, the mindset of English administration in India was only concentrated on revenue generation and/or criminal law for law and order. They never were concerned with the ground level approach of the Hindus. Thus, took an easy way out and dismissed.

In December 1949, 50-60 people placed the idols of Ram and several other objects right under the central dome, consequently, leading the property going into the hands of the receiver, and puja being conducted by a Pujari appointed by the receiver. In furtherance, on 16 January 1950 Gopal Singh Visharad had filed a Suit in the Fiazabad Civil Court seeking exclusive rights for performing Puja for Ram Lalla, also prayed for temporary injunction which was granted and was confirmed by a division bench of the Hon'ble Allahabad High Court. (registered as Suit No.1). later that year in December, Mahant Paramahansa Ramchandra Das, had filed a suit for the continuation of Puja and keeping the idols in the Babri structure. But subsequently, the same was withdrawn. (registered as Suit No.2). on December 17th, 1959 Suit no. 3 was filed by Nirmohi Akhara seeking transfer of charge of the dispute site from the receiver. On 18 December 1961 Suit no. 4

was filed by U.P Sunni Central Board of Waqfs for declaration and possession of the Disputed site. In 1984, we could see the activation of the movement to build the Grand Ram Temple Ayodhya. In February, 1986 order was passed by the Faizabad District Judge for opening locks of the Ram Janmabhoomi Site and allowing Puja by devotees. A committee was formulated of Prominent Muslim leaders called the Babri Masjid Action Committee. Two days after the lock was opened, a petition was filed on any further development at the site. The Hon'ble Judge issued a notice that the "Status quo" be maintained. On 9 November, 1989 also with only days to go for the Lok-Sabha Elections, the Rajiv Gandhi Government allowed the VHP (Vishva Hindu Parishad) to perform the shilanyas (foundation laying ceremony) of the temple. On 1st july 1989, Suit no. 5 was filed in the name of Baghwan Ram Lalla Virajman. In the same year, on an application by the then Advocate General of U.P., these Suits were transferred to the High Court. During 1990, L.K. Advani's Ram Rath Yatra was also witnessed. After that we saw the introduction and withdrawal of the Ram Janmabhoomi/ Babri masjid (Acquisition of area) Ordinance, 1990 promulgated to acquire the disputed shrine and its adjoining area.

On 6 December 1992, Ram Janmabhoomi/Babri Masjid was attacked and shattered. The idols were removed and reinstalled. President's rule was immediately imposed in Uttar Pradesh and State Assembly was dissolved. It was decided by the union Government to take over the entire land. To that effect, on 7 January 1993 acquisition of certain area at ayodhya ordinance issued. Constitutionality of the Act was challenged and a bench of five judges started deliberations in September 1993. In 1994, in M. Ismail Faruqui Vs. Union of India [(1994)

VI SCC 360] the Hon'ble Supreme Court by a majority decision upheld the law acquiring the land. The same was challenged in 2018 to refer it to a larger bench but the same was turned down by a bench led by the then Chief Justice of India Hon'ble Dipak Misra (AIR 2018 SC 5134). In the above-mentioned case, the Hon'ble Supreme Court held that a mosque is not an essential part or integral part of the practice of the religion of Islam and Namaz. (Prayers) by Muslims can be offered anywhere, even in open. And accordingly, its acquisition is not prohibited by the provisions in the Constitution of India. In 2018, also the bench had noticed that the Constitutional bench in 1994 had held that acquisition is a sovereign or prerogative power of the state to acquire property and all religious places, namely, church, mosque, temple etc. are liable to be acquired in exercise of right of eminent domain of the State. Further, held that if a particular place is of such significance for that religion that worship at such place is an essential religious practice and the extinction of such place may breach their right of Article 25, the acquisition of such place is not permissible.

The judgement commences with detecting the background of the issue, thereby extracting facts from White Paper (published by the Central Government). Paragraph 1.1 of the paper published by the Central Government explains the significance of the Ayodhya district, which has been a place of holy pilgrimage because of its mention in the epic Ramayan as the place of birth of Shri Ram. Further, the Bhoomi is believed that it is the birthplace of Shri Ram where a temple stood earlier, where masjid was erected in 1528 AD. Paragraph 1.2 of the same document illustrates the phase of the polemic, when idols where placed in December 1949. Subsequently, the property was attached under Section 145 of the CrPC. Thereafter, Civil

Suits were filed to which interim orders were passed for restraining the parties from amputating the idols or meddling with their worship. So, from December 1949 to 6th December 1992, the configuration had not been used as a Mosque. Additionally, the Judgment tracks down the inception of the Undertaking to paradigm an Ostentatious Ram-Temple at the Disputed Site. After certain failed parleys involving VHP and AIBMAC, in June 1991, a new Government of BJP was formed in the State of Uttar Pradesh with a declaration of a commitment toward the construction of the Ram-Temple. The same was began, with acquisition of certain Undisputed-Land, adjoining the disputed land. The emphasis was to build the Ram-Temple at the bhoomi where Ram was born called the Ram-Janmbhoomi through temple construction movement by way of Kar-Sewa [Selfless service to others]. Subsequently, demolishing of the Dome-Structure. The judgment tags the demolishing as a "National-Shame" while shaking the faith of minority in the rule of law. The bench led-by the then CJI Dipak Misra noticed more details of suits, which were filed in the year 1950 and thereafter, which suits were ultimately transferred to the Allahabad High Court to be heard together in the year 1989. The judgment further while tracking down the history of the issue and mentions, the Proclamation under Article 356 of the Constitution of India passed after 06.12.1992, and therefore acquiring all areas in the dispute in the suits pending in the Allahabad High Court. To this, an ordinance was passed and issued on 07.01.1993 called namely, "The Acquisition of Certain Areas at Ayodhya Ordinance." To the effect, 67.703 acres of land in the complex was acquired by the Central Government. The ordinance No. 8 of 1993 was then replaced by the Acquisition of certain areas at Ayodhya act, 1993 (No. 33

of 1993). The instant judgment [M. Ismail Faruqui Vs. Union of India [(1994) VI SCC 360 and in reference to a larger bench i.e. AIR 2018 SC 5134] was the outcome of a Writ Petition under Article 32 filed in the Apex Court. The majority of the judgment upheld the validly of the Act, except that of Section 4(3) of the Act of 1993 which was struck down. Subsequent to this, one petition was filed in the Apex Court by Moh. Aslam. The Apex Court, passed an "interim" order/judgment (31.03.2003) to restrain Government to hand-over any part of the entire complex to any party and also restrained all/ any form of religious activity of any kind by anyone to take place until disposal of the suits in the High Court of Allahabad [(2003) IV SCC 1]. The same was only operative till the adjudication of the High Court of Allahabad. Now, it is infructuous. The argument proposed by the Ld. Advocate for the Plaintiff of Suit No. 4 with respect to the Judgment of 1994 of mosque not an essential part of the practice of the religious of Islam and Namaz (prayer) by Muslim can be offered anywhere, even in open referring to a larger bench was that whether essential practice can be decided on a mere ipse dixit [an assertion without proof] of the Court or whether the Court is obliged to examine belief, tenets and practice, is a pure question of law. The 1994 devoid of any examination on the tis issue, the matter requires a larger bench reference. Shri. K. Parasaran, Ld. Senior Advocate refuted the argument proposed by the Ld. Advocate for plaintiff of Suit No. 4, claimed and submitted that the interests of the Muslim Community were adequately represented before the Court in the Case in contention. Further, submitted that the Judgment is binding on those who are eo -nomine [under that name] parties thereto. Furthermore, submitting to the court that even apart from the question of res judicata, the doctrine of representation binds those whose interests are the same in the subject matter of

Ram-Janmabhomi-Babri Majid dispute as those of eo-nomine parties. In the judgment, the bench also notices the significance of the district of Ayodhya as a place of pilgrimage because of the antediluvian belief that Lord Ram was born there. The Court held and penned that Article 25 of the Constitution of India i.e. Fundamental right to practice, profess and propagate religion does not include the right to acquire or own or possess property unless the place has a particular significance. In the instant case the place where Lord ram was born is of a certain significance established and the temple set-up is according to Pranaprathistha Puja and according to Agama Shastra. Therefore, on comparison in terms of sacredness and essentiality, mosque and temple cannot be at par. In a temple, in which the idol has been consecrated by Pranaprathistha Puja and built according to Agama Shastra's is of Religious significance. The Rama idol on the Chabutra is one such consecrated. In this judgment [para 105], the commitment of the Cabinet Committee of the then Prime Minister's recorded by the Hon'ble Supreme Court which is a binding commitment. A temple and a masjid cannot be considered on par as far as sacredness is concerned. A masjid is not an essential part of the Islamic religion, according to the above majority judgement of a Constitution Bench of the Supreme Court; and theocratic Islamic Countries such as Saudi Arabia do demolish mosques for public purposes. In Masjid Shahid Ganj v. Shiromani Gurdwara Prabandhak Committee, Amritsar AIR 1938 Lahore 369 (FB), [also part of the above said judgment] it was held that where a mosque has been adversely possessed by non-Muslims, it lost its sacred character as mosque. The Hon'ble Supreme Court upheld the validity of Ismail Farooqui vs Union of India [(1994) 6 SCC 360] while making the observation regarding a claim of immunity of a mosque from acquisition. Furthermore, the disputed area is of a particular significance to Hindus thus any hindrance to offer prayer herein is in violation of the access to worship at the place where his God was born, which fundamental right is Author's Fundamental Right to pray guaranteed under the Constitution of India under Article 25 and 26. The Hon'ble Court in the 2018 judgment, unequivocally laid down that every immovable property is liable to be acquired under the concept enriched in the Constitution of India. In the end, it was clear that the questionable observations made in Ismail Faruqi's case were made in context of land acquisition.

Excavation at the disputed site of Ram-Janmabhoomi-Babri Majid was carried out by the Archeological Survey of India (ASI) from 12th March 2003 to 7th August 2003. This excavation was carried out in pursuance of an order to get sufficient archaeological evidence on the issues involved "whether there was any temple/structure which was demolished and mosque was constructed on the disputed site," the Hon'ble Lucknow Bench of the Allahabad High Court had given directions to ASI to excavate at the disputed site where the GPR Survey had suggested evidence of anomalies which could be structure, pillars, foundation walls slab flooring etc. which could be confirmed by excavation. To summaries the ASI while viewing the entire survey in toto and taking into account the archeological evidence of continuity in structural phases from the tenth century onwards up to the construction of the disputed structure along with the yield of stone and decorated bricks as well as mutilated sculpture of divine couple and carved architectural members including foliage patterns, amalaka, kapotapali doorjamb with semi-circular pilaster, broken octagonal shaft of black schist pillar, lotus motif, circular shrine having pranala (waterchute) in the north, fifty pillar bases in association of the huge structure, are indicative of remains which are distinctive features found associated with the temples of North India. [Pg 3851 of the HC judgement]. By July 2010, arguments were concluded before the Lucknow Bench of the Allahabad high court and had set a date 30 September 2010 to deliver the verdict. One more observation of the High Court of Allahabad in the verdict is also that a structure having images/ idols and designs of and portraits of living things cannot be a mosque under law of sharia: As such the disputed structure cannot be termed as a mosque at all: The Holy Prophet has said that angels do not enter in a house which has images, portraits, pictures, idols etc., and even garments with such designs detract attention from prayer and, for that reason it is prohibited to decorate a mosque with such pictures. As the disputed structure on its columns and other load bearing parts had engraved/ chiseled images/idols of Yakshas, Devis, Divine-couples, Kalash, Lotus, Leaves, Varah, Swastiks, Srivatsa, Kapot-pallis, etc. it cannot come within the definition of Masjid according to Muslim Religious Law and belief but it comes within the definition of a Hindu Temple according to Hindu Personal Religious Law and belief. The Bench decided to equally divide the disputed land between the three main litigants—which meant 2/3rd of the land to Hindu parties and 1/3rd to Muslim parties. The same was rejected and an appeal was filed, demanding for claim to the entire land.

RECORD OF TALKS (BETWEEN HINDUS AND MUSLIMS)

The Vishva Hindu Parishad [VHP] tried all media and fora of talks in order that the Muslim leaders of India would know, understand, appreciate and respect the feelings, sentiments and beliefs of the Hindu society. But the experience was that the Muslim leadership was not interested in ending this age-old struggle and starting a new era of mutual trust and harmony. During the period of Late Prime Minister Shri Rajiv Gandhi, Sri Buta Singhji and Mrs. Sheila Dixit used to mediate. In Delhi itself, several mediation sessions took place across the table. Once Ven. Swami Satyamitranand ji Maharaj was alsoin the meeting! It was noon time and a Friday—the sixth and most important day in Islamic week—and it was time to offer the Prayer of Jummah.

When the gentlemen of the Muslim side returned after offering Namaz, Ven. Swami Satyamitranand ji Maharaj stood up and spreading his monk's robe said: 'Salat (prayer/namaz) is followed by Zakat (alms-giving). I beg of you Sri Ram's birthplace as alms!" The Namazis kept their mouths shut and their total silence spoke volumes about their intentions. Maharajshree sat down. During another mediation talk, Syed Shahabuddin had offered that if it was proved that after demolishing a temple the mosque was constructed, then they would voluntarily handover the site to the Hindus. This promise is recorded in the White Paper published by the Government of India. This Para No. 2.3 of White Paper is also quoted / mentioned by the SCI in the Ismail Faruqi judgment (as 2.8, which is wrongly typed). Bilateral talks started on the initiative of the Government of India during the tenure of Shri Chandrashekharji as Prime Minister. The then GOI Minister of State for Home, Shri Subodh Kant Sahai, the then Chief Ministers of Uttar Pradesh, Maharashtra and Rajasthan, Mulayam Singh Yadav, Sharad Pawar and Bhairon Singh Shekhawat respectively also used to remain present in these meetings. On 01 December 1990, representatives of Government and VHP met held talks met at a residence in Mathura Road. Union Law Minister Dr. Subramanian Swamy and VHP Vice President Giriraj Kishore agreed that the 9 December 1990 proposed VHP karseva in Ayodhya be postponed, and further talks with a formal team be continued on a possible compromise settlement arrived at in back channel talks between Dr. Swamy and Syed Shahbuddin during November 1990. A suggestion came that a time limit be set for an amicable resolution of the dispute. It was then decided that:

1. Both parties should provide their respective evidences to the Minister of State for Home by 22 December 1990.
2. Copies of the evidences be made available to all concerned by 25 December 1990.
3. After verification and attestation of these evidences, the two sides again would meet on 10 January 1991 at 10.00 a.m.

A formal document of the bilateral talks was thus prepared in the office of the Minister of State for Home Affairs. The evidences of each other were to be responded/rejoindered to by 6 January 1991. The Vishva Hindu Parishad responded by dismissing the claims of the Babri Masjid Action Committee. Whereas, instead of giving any rejoinder to VHP's evidences that bolstered its case, only photocopies of some additional evidences were given by the Babri Committee to further prove their stand. In the absence of any rejoinder from the Babri Committee, it became difficult for the government to find out what were the points of agreement and disagreement. A meeting was held on 10 January 1991 at Gujarat Bhavan. It was decided that the documents presented should be classified under Historical, Archaeological, Revenue and Law categories. It was also decided that both sides would give the names of their experts, who would study the relevant documents and then meet on 24 and 25 January 1991 and give their comments by 5 February 1991. Thereafter, both sides would reconsider the reports of these experts. The Babri Masjid Committee suddenly started dodging maneuvers. The committee did not name its experts. They continued to change their list of experts. Among the experts who came on 24 January 1991, four were the executive officers of Babri Masjid Action Committee and Dr. R.S. Sharma, Dr. D. N. Jha, Dr. Surajbhan and Dr. M. Athar Ali were experts. Present, on behalf of the VHP, were legal luminaries like Justice Guman Mal Lodha, Justice Deoki Nandan Agarwal, Justice Dharamveer Sahgal and Senior Advocate Shri Virendra Kumar Singh Chaudhury, and present as historians and revenue experts were Dr Harshnarain, Prof. B.R. Grover, Prof. K.S. Lal, Prof. B.P. Sinha, Prof. Devendra Swarup Agarwal and Archaeologist Dr S.P. Gupta. At the outset, the experts of the Babri Committee said that they had neither visited Ayodhya nor studied the evidence and said that they needed at least six weeks for it. This happened on 24 January 1991. The Babri Committee experts did not turn up for the meeting scheduled on 25th January while representatives and experts of the VHP waited for two hours. The same story repeated in the subsequent meeting. The talks finally stopped. Even in October-November 1992, correspondence took place between Vishva Hindu Parishad and the Babri Masjid Action Committee. The result turned out to be zero.

TIME LINE OF CONFLICTS AND OF MOVEMENTS

(*i*) The struggle to get back the birthplace continues unabated since 1528 CE (since the day invader Babur ordered demolition of the temple and superimposition of the triple-domed Jihadi statement/structure over it).

(*ii*) The entire Hindu society has incessantly been waging this fight. The saint fraternity of Ayodhya and the kings/ emperors of the areas around have had special contributions in this fight back.

(*iii*) The pages of history record details of 76 battles for this cause.

(*iv*) The history of battles speaks volumes about the fact that Hindus never ever gave up their claim over this place.

(*v*) These battles and struggles show that the occupation of this place by the Muslim invader and his descendants was never peaceful, continuous, uninterrupted.

(*vi*) In 1885 CE, an application was moved before the then government official on behalf of Nirmohi Akhara with a request to permit replacement of the thatched canopy by a concrete one above the Ramchabutra (raised-platform) located in the outer courtyard of the birthplace complex. On this subject, the British Judge Colonel FEA Chamier (Faizabad District Judge) declined permission, but in his verdict admitted that "...It is most unfortunate that a masjid should have been built on the land specially held sacred by the Hindus..."

(*vii*) At the Hindu Conference held at Muzaffarnagar in Uttar Pradesh in March 1983, the late Dau Dayal Khanna, a former Congress minister and U.P. State legislator, called upon the Ram devotees to "liberate the places of Ayodhya, Mathura and Kashi and bring back the glory of Hindustan."

(*viii*) On 7 and 8 April 1984, a conference of saints took place at Vigyan Bhawan, New Delhi (First Dharma Sansad/ Dharma Parliament). The Dharma Sansad prescribed and mandated the liberation of the Sri Ram Janma Bhumi at Ayodhya. Thus, with the directive of the Sant Fraternity, the Vishva Hindu Parishad started the 77th edition of the five centuries old struggle.

(*ix*) The new struggle and pan-India movement was initiated by a public awareness campaign to open the locks put on the birthplace. The Ram-Janaki chariot was consecrated at Sitamarhi. On October 07, 1984, the Ram-Janaki Rath arrived at the banks of the Holy Saryu River in Ayodhya. Thousands of Ram devotees took Saryu Maharani's sacred waters in hand and vowed to liberate the Sri Ram Janma Bhumi.

(*x*) From October, 1985, public awareness campaign started again in Uttar Pradesh by 6 chariots under the banner of Ram Janma Bhumi Mukti Rath Yatra. As a result, the locks put on the Sri Ram's Birthplace in the year 1949 CE were opened on 1 February 1986 by order of the court. There were several attempts made to stop public worship and prayers to Ramlala, but the court did not accept it.

(*xi*) After this, a series of public awareness campaigns started. The Ram Shila Pujan (consecration of clay, stone or marble bricks) programmes were organized in about 300,000 villages across the country. Consecrated bricks from across the country and abroad reached Ayodhya. In the presence of the revered saints and sages, the first foundation stone was laid for the grand Ram temple as per Hindu aspirations by Shri Kameshwar Chowpal, a Karyakarta/worker from amongst the Scheduled Castes brethren. This event was a wonderful example of the united strength of the Ram devotees as well as that of social harmony.

(*xii*) Many programs like Ram Jyoti, Ramcharan Paduka Pujan, Vijay Mantra Jaap Abhiyan led to a unique awakening in the country.

(*xiii*) On 24 June 1990, in Haridwar, in a meeting of the Kendriya Margdarshak Mandal it was decided to go to Ayodhya to perform Karseva on 30 October 1990 (Devotthan Ekadashi). The then Chief Minister of Uttar Pradesh made tricky cordon off plans around Ayodhya to plug up all entry points whatsoever to make Ayodhya out of bounds for all incoming devotees and declared that 'Not even a bird/avian can dare flap its wings here'. The Hindu society accepted this challenge and thousands of people managed to brave or tiptoe and/or creep into the town of Ayodhya from all directions despite all kinds of repression from police. The Karsevaks (volunteers) hoisted the saffron flags on the domes at the appointed time. Police firings martyred karsevaks. The firing incident of 2 November 1990 is known by all. At the end of the day, the government bowed down and all the kar sevaks got permission to have darshan, and only then they returned home.

(*xiv*) Ten days of Satyagraha took place; thousands of people came every day. The ashes of the martyred Karsevaks were taken around the country and millions of people paid their homage to it.

(*xv*) On 4 April 1991, the historic Virat Hindu Sammelan was held at the Boat Club, New Delhi. An estimated 25 lakh (2½ million) Rama devotees attended this meeting. Even as the meeting was to conclude, the Chief Minister of Uttar Pradesh, Mulayam Singh Yadav resigned. There were re-elections in Uttar Pradesh, Sri Kalyan Singh became the Chief Minister.

(*xvi*) It was announced again that the Karseva would take place on 6 December 1992. Sri Kalyan Singh Ji announced that bullets won't be fired. Security forces were stationed around Ayodhya. The pent-up feelings of the society burst out due to the atrocities on the Ram devotees and fortuitously the Babri structure got deconstructed.

(*xvii*) Millions of Ram devotees participated in this phase of the Ram Janma Bhumi struggle started from 1984 CE. The resolve of the Ram devotees became stronger with every campaign.

(*xviii*) **THE SUPREME COURT MONITORED MEDIATION:** In February 2019, the Hon'ble Supreme Court of India expressed a desire that the parties involved engage in mutual talks to iron out differences and explore a mutually acceptable solution to the dispute. In March 2019, the SCI entrusted the task to a three-member Mediation Committee comprising of (1) Justice (Rtd. SCI) Ibrahim Kalifulla (Chennai), (2) Senior Advocate of Madras High Court, Shri Sriram Panchu, (3) Art of Living Founder Sri Sri Ravi Shankar. The Mediation Committee held talks separately with all parties concerned between 13 March 2019 and 1 August 2019 in seven rounds at Ayodhya. All the talks were kept confidential. The mediators offered thanks to everyone on 1 August 2019, and on 2 August as they presented their mediation termination letter to the Hon'ble Supreme Court. Even this talks attempt proved unsuccessful. Subsequently, on 2 August, the Hon'ble Supreme Court ordered regular hearing of appeals from 6 August, and also said that from Monday to Friday, work will be done 5 days a week and daily from 10.30 am to 4.00 pm. Verbally it said that they would work on

Saturdays also as per requirement, or after 4:00 pm, do one-hour extra work. A total of 40 days of arguments were heard from 6 August to 16 October 2019. The last 11 working days saw one extra hour of work every day. A total of 170 hours of work was done in 40 days. Additionally, on 16 October 2019, the Constitution Bench declared the hearing complete and gave a written order that all parties should give their respective written submissions in the next three days in relation to moulding of relief or alternative relief they sought if the primary relief of title/ownership was not granted to them.

CHAPTER 3

Faith and Fundamental Rights: The Basis

Security to authors' liberty of Faith, Belief and Worship is enshrined in the basic structure of the Constitution of India. The same faith divulges authors that Lord Ram was born at the same spot which was is called "The Ram-Janmbhoomi" at Ayodhya. According to the faith of a billion plus Hindu Bhakts in India and abroad, this is the exact area where Lord Ram was born; and thus, it remains firmly identified in their minds and held as sacred. These objectives are part of the Basic Structure of the Constitution. The Concept of the Basic Structure has been dealt by the Hon'ble Supreme Court in depth in Keshavananda Bharati vs. State of Kerala: 1973 (Suppl Vol 1) SCR paras 292, 437, 599, 682 and 1164; and Minerva Mills Ltd vs. Union of India: 1980 (1) SCR 206]. As a fundamental right guaranteed under Article 25 of the Constitution of India, it includes for Hindus the Right to Pray in particular to have access to due worship at the place where faith determines is the place where their God was born. In contrast the Mosque site is/has of no such essential significance for Muslims. [(1994) 6 SCC 376]. In the above-mentioned case, the Hon'ble Supreme Court held that a mosque is not an essential part or integral part of the practice of the religion of Islam and Namaz. (Prayers) by Muslims can be offered anywhere, even in open. And accordingly, its acquisition is not prohibited by the provisions in the Constitution of India. The same was challenged in 2018 to refer it to a larger bench but the same was turned down by a bench led by the then Chief Justice of India Hon'ble Dipak Misra [AIR 2018 SC 5134]. In 2018, also the bench had noticed that the Constitutional bench in 1994 had held that acquisition is a sovereign or prerogative power of the state to acquire property and all religious places, namely, church, mosque, temple etc. are liable to be acquired in exercise of right of eminent domain of the State. Further, held that if a particular place is of such significance for that religion that worship at such place is an essential religious practice and the extinction of such place may breach their right of Article 25, the acquisition of such place is not permissible.

The judgement in 2018, commences with detecting the background of the issue, thereby extracting facts from White Paper [published by the Central Government]. Paragraph 1.1 of the paper published by the Central Government explains the significance of the Ayodhya district, which has been a place of holy pilgrimage because of its mention in the epic Ramayan as the place of birth of Shri Ram. Further, the Bhoomi is believed that it is the birthplace of Shri Ram where a temple stood earlier, where masjid was erected in 1528 AD. Paragraph 1.2 of the same document illustrates the phase of the polemic, when idols where placed in December 1949. Subsequently, the property was attached under Section 145 of the CrPC. Thereafter, Civil Suits were filed to which interim orders were passed for restraining the parties from amputating the idols or meddling with their worship. So, from December 1949 to 6 December 1992, the configuration had not been used as a Mosque. Additionally, the Judgment tracks down the inception of the Undertaking to paradigm an Ostentatious Ram-Temple at the Disputed Site. After certain failed parleys involving VHP and AIBMAC, in June 1991, a new Government of BJP was formed in the State of Uttar Pradesh with a declaration of a commitment toward the construction of the Ram-Temple. The same was began, with acquisition of certain Undisputed-Land, adjoining the disputed land. The emphasis was to build the Ram-Temple at the bhoomi where Ram was born called the Ram-Janmbhoomi through temple construction movement by way of Kar-Sewa [Selfless service to others]. Subsequently, demolishing of the Dome-Structure. The judgment tags the demolishing as a "National-Shame" while shaking the faith of minority in the rule of law. The bench led-by the then CJI Dipak Misra noticed more details of suits, which were filed in the year 1950 and thereafter, which suits were ultimately transferred to the Allahabad High Court to be heard together in the year 1989. The judgment further while tracking down the history of the issue and mentions, the Proclamation under Article 356 of the Constitution of India passed after 06.12.1992, and therefore acquiring all areas in the dispute in the suits pending in the Allahabad High Court. To this, an ordinance was passed and issued on 07.01.1993 called namely, "The Acquisition of Certain Areas at Ayodhya Ordinance." To the effect, 67.703 acres of land in the complex was acquired by the Central Government. The ordinance No. 8 of 1993 was then replaced by the Acquisition of certain areas at Ayodhya act, 1993 (No. 33 of 1993). The instant judgment [M. Ismail Faruqui Vs. Union of India [(1994) VI SCC 360 and in reference to a larger bench i.e. AIR 2018 SC 5134] was the outcome of a Writ Petition under Article 32 filed in the Apex Court. The majority of the judgment upheld the validly of the Act, except that of Section 4(3) of the Act of 1993 which was struck down. Subsequent to this, one petition was filed in the Apex Court by Moh. Aslam. The Apex Court, passed an "interim" order/judgment (31.03.2003) to restrain Government to hand-over any part of the entire complex to any party and also restrained all/ any form of religious activity of any kind by anyone to take place until disposal of the suits in the High Court of Allahabad [(2003) IV SCC 1].

The same was only operative till the adjudication of the High Court of Allahabad. Now, it is infructuous. The argument proposed by the Advocate of plaintiff of Suit No. 4 with respect to the Judgment of 1994 of mosque not an essential part of the practice of the religious of Islam and Namaz (prayer) by Muslim can be offered anywhere, even in open referring to a larger bench was that whether essential practice can be decided on a mere *ipse dixit* [an assertion without proof] of the Court or whether the Court is obliged to examine belief, tenets and practice, is a pure question of law. The 1994 devoid of any examination on the tis issue, the matter requires a larger bench reference. Shri. K. Parasaran, Ld. Senior Advocate refuted the argument proposed by the Advocate of plaintiff of Suit No. 4, claimed and submitted that the interests of the Muslim Community were adequately represented before the Court in the Case in contention. Further, submitted that the Judgment is binding on those who are eo-nomine [under that name] parties thereto. Furthermore, submitting to the court that even apart from the question of res judicata, the doctrine of representation binds those whose interests are the same in the subject matter of Ram-Janmabhomi-Babri Majid dispute as those of eo-nomine parties. In the judgment, the bench also notices the significance of the district of Ayodhya as a place of pilgrimage because of the antediluvian belief that Lord Ram was born there. The Court held and penned that Article 25 of the Constitution of India i.e. Fundamental right to practice, profess and propagate religion does not include the right to acquire or own or possess property unless the place has a particular significance. In the instant case the place where Lord ram was born is of a certain significance established and the temple set-up is according to Pranaprathistha Puja and according to Agama Shastra. Therefore, on comparison in terms of sacredness and essentiality, mosque and temple cannot be at par. In a temple, in which the idol has been consecrated by Pranaprathistha Puja and built according to Agama Shastra's is of Religious significance. The Rama idol on the Chabutra is one such consecrated. In this judgment [para 105], the commitment of the Cabinet Committee of the then Prime Minister's recorded by the Hon'ble Supreme Court which is a binding commitment. A temple and a masjid cannot be considered on par as far as sacredness is concerned. A masjid is not an essential part of the Islamic religion, according to the above majority judgement of a Constitution Bench of the Supreme Court; and theocratic Islamic Countries such as Saudi Arabia do demolish mosques for public purposes. In Masjid Shahid Ganj v. Shiromani Gurdwara Prabandhak Committee, Amritsar AIR 1938 Lahore 369 (FB), [also part of the above said judgment] it was held that where a mosque has been adversely possessed by non-Muslims, it lost its sacred character as mosque. The Hon'ble Supreme Court upheld the validity of Ismail Farooqui vs Union of India [(1994) 6 SCC 360] while making the observation regarding a claim of immunity of a mosque from acquisition. Furthermore, the disputed area is of a particular significance to Hindus thus any hindrance to offer prayer herein is in violation of the access to worship at the place where his God was born, which fundamental right is Author's Fundamental Right to pray guaranteed under the Constitution of India under Article 25 and 26. The Hon'ble Court in the 2018 judgment, unequivocally laid down that every immovable property is liable to be acquired under the concept enriched in the Constitution of India. In the end, it was clear that questionable observation made in Ismail Faruqi's case were made in context of land acquisition. There is a fundamental theological difference between reading namaz in a mosque and worshipping at a temple which is built according to the Agama Shastra and constructed after performing Prana Prathista Puja at the Garbha Graha. It is also most respectfully submitted that Namaz can be read anywhere, including not only in a mosque built as a prayer hall, but even on the roads, railway platform or on an airplane, and hence the Sharia law as practiced in any theocratic Islamic nation permits mosques to be shifted or demolished by the appropriate governments for a public purpose. This happens regularly in Saudi Arabia, Iran, Pakistan and other Islamic countries.

The Right to Practice under Article 25 enshrined under part III [Basic Structure] of the Constitution of India and read with the Security of liberty of faith, belief and Worship enshrined under the Preamble, Hindu religion includes due access to duly offer due prayers bereft of unreasonable restrictions at a place identified by all devotees, as a matter of faith, as the birthplace [or janmasthan] of Lord Ram. Fundamental Right of the Authors' to pray at the same spot where faith tells that Lord Ram was born referred to as Ram Jamnabhoomi has always superseded when compared to a mere property right as Right to property is no longer a fundamental right after the deletion of Article 19(1)(f) and Article 31 from the Constitution of India Vide the 44th Amendment, 1978.

This is the faith of Hindus and the same can also be substantiated through numerous texts, including the Valmiki Ramayana, Atharava Veda, Yajurveda, Skanda Purana And Goswami Tulsidas. It is submitted that the description found in these texts confirms the disputed site in Ayodhya as being the birth place of Lord Ram. Furthermore, in the "Tulsi Doha Shatak" of Tulsi Das, there is a mention about construction of mosque on command of Babar by Mir Baqi after demolishing the Sri Ram-Janmabhoomi. That the "Kavitavali" composed by Goswami Tulsidas contains reference of the excesses and atrocities committed by the Mughal Emperors and the "Dohawali" composed by him elucidates the political, cultural hegemony and situation at that point of time. Valmiki's Ramayana is a very old and recognized treatise of the Hindus, composed during the times of Lord Ram. In "Sarg" (chapter) 18 of "Balkaand" Valmiki Ramayana, Maharshi Valmiki has described the birth of Lord Sri Ramchandra along with the relevant time of birth, season, planet position etc and he has described the birthplace by the term "Sarvlok Namaskritam." Ayodhya and Ram-Janmabhoomi and their importance, are also mentioned in "Vaishnava" part of "Skanda Purana." The following extract is reproduced as: "on the North-east of that place lies Ram-Janmabhoomi (where at present Ram-Lalla is presiding). The same Ram-Janmabhoomi is known as Ram-Janmabhoomi or expressed in the said manner and it is a provider of liberation, etc. That this resolves to make the belief of Hindus true with a firm conviction as trustworthy. The disputed structure on its columns and other load bearing parts had engraved/chiseled images/idols of Yakshas, Devis, Divine-couples, Kalash, Lotus, Leaves, Varah, Swastiks, Srivatsa, Kapot-pallis, etc. A structure having images/idols and designs of and portraits of living things cannot be a mosque under law of sharia: As such the disputed structure cannot be termed as a mosque at all, but it comes within the definition of a Hindu Temple according to Hindu Personal Religious Law and belief. There is no dispute between the parties that there were 14 pillars inside and outside the disputed structure. As set out in detail by the Parties in the Civil Appeals [in C.A. No. 4768-4771/2011 connected with C.A. 10866-10877/2010], prior to the demolition of the disputed structure there existed photographs of these pillars. In all the 30 photographs thereof, there are certain images of Hindu Gods and Goddesses and religious marks on these pillars. This has been confirmed and accepted by the Hon'ble Lower Court, the Allahabad High Court (Lucknow Bench) [Citation: 2010 ADJ 1 (Special. F.B)]. In fact, as such a building decorated with such pictures cannot be declared as a Masjid.

Now, elucidating on the Religious position of Temple interpreted by Foreign Courts, it clarifies the fortified position of Temples with respect to Hindu beliefs and Faith enriched in the Preamble. Emerging from the Judgment of the English Court of Appeals in the Bumper Development Corp Ltd Vs. Commissioner of Police and other claimants [(1991) 4 AII ER 638] and of the suit from which it arose, that a temple (through its trustees) is always a temple even if in disuse or ruins. [judgment in the Trial Court was delivered by Justice Ian Kennedy]. The Judgement further sheds light on the principle that a temple holds its position secured even if it is in disuse or in ruins and it is considered as a temple with deity residing in the temple. The idol installed through Agama Shastra and after Pranaprathistha Puja is a juristic person to sue for recovery. Thus, it is legally tenable to state that Hindu Worshippers at the Ram Temple on Ram-Janmabhoomi always had an overriding fundamental right to pray at the site, which right is superior to the claim of the parties claiming for restoration of Babri mosque as a right to property.

The well understood and agreed concept of Faith is defined for instance in the Court of Civil Appeals of Texas in Daniel vs.

Modern Woodmen of America [53 Tex. Civ. App. 570] (which cites the definition of Webster's unabridged dictionary) as: "a firm conviction of the truth of what is declared by another by way either of testimony or authority without other evidence; belief in what another states, affirms, or testifies simply on the ground of his truth or veracity; especially (as distinguished from mere belief) practical dependence on a person, statement or thing as trustworthy." This is the faith of Hindus and the same can also be substantiated through numerous texts, including the Valmiki Ramayana, Atharava Veda, Yajurveda, Skanda Purana And Goswami Tulsidas. It is submitted that the description found in these texts confirms the disputed site in Ayodhya as being the birth place of Lord Ram. The fundamental rights of Hindus under Article 25 of the Constitution of India are superior to the title rights being allegedly claimed by the Muslims; Bhagwan Ram's birthplace at Ayodhya is established as expressed by the Court in the following terms on the basis of convincing epigraphical evidence the belief of Hindus and the arguments advanced by Hindus, I am of the view that the city of Ayodhya undeniably is city of great antiquity and sacred spot to the Hindus for a long time. Valmiki Ramayan, Srimad Bhagwat, Mahabhart and Raghuvansham recognized the identity of Ayodhya.

The Principle of faith and its proper protection were upheld and elucidated by the Hon'ble US Supreme Court in *Masterpiece Cakeshop Ltd., et al vs. Colorado Civil Rights Commission* [584 U.S. _____(2018) No. 16-111]. The Relevant Paragraph is reproduced below:

> *"At the same time, the religious and philosophical objections to gay marriage are protected views and, in some instances, protected forms of expression. As this Court observed in Obergefell v. Hodges,*

*576 U. S______(2015), "[T]**he First Amendment ensures that religious organizations and persons are given proper protection as they seek to teach the principles that are so fulfilling and so central to their lives and faiths.**" Id., at (slip op., at 27)."*

"... Nor would it be proper for this or any court to suggest that a person must be forced to write words rather than create a symbol before his religious faith is implicated. Civil authorities, whether "high or petty," bear no license to declare what is or should be "orthodox" when it comes to religious beliefs, id., at 642, or whether an adherent has "correctly perceived" the commands of his religion, Thomas, supra, at 716. ***Instead, it is our job to look beyond the formality of written words and afford legal protection to any sincere act of faith.***"

[Emphasis Supplied]

Such principles of acceptance and respect for a faith, deeply and widely held is not peculiar only to the Hindu belief that the Ram-Janmabhoomi area is where there is the birthplace of Lord Rama. Cited herein below are other holy sites widely believed in and worshipped at by followers of Christianity and Islam.

1. The Dome of The Rock in Jerusalam
2. The Church of The Nativity and the Pilgrimage Route in Bethlehem
3. The Church of The Holy Sepulchre in Jerusalem.

Building upon the Right to pray is a Fundamental Right and a temple built according to Agama Shastras and following the Prana Prathista Puja is always a temple; it is a criminal offence if such a place which is "held sacred" is destroyed or hurt. That any such act which is initiated to destroying, injuring or defiling any such place of Worship which is held scared is a Criminal Act penalized under the Indian Penal Code, 1860,

Section 295 of the Act. The Legislature has, in its wisdom used the word "held" to connote that it is concerned with the subjective belief of people and there this fact does not require any objective proof. In the present scenario, it is an article of faith, an unique and express belief of all Hindus that Lord Ram was born at the Ram Janmabhoomi and it is undisputed in that there is no myth, literature or scientific study states that any other place was Lord Ram place of birth. Thus, this is a unique and incontrovertible belief of Hindus. The Apex Court of Law, has also interpreted the Section 295 of the Indian Penal Code, 1860 in S. Veerabadran Chettiar Vs. E.V. Ramaswami Nacker & ors. [AIR 1958 SC 1032] and held:

> *"7....Any object however trivial or destitute of real value in itself, if regarded as sacred by any class of persons would come within the meaning of the penal section. Nor is it absolutely necessary that the object, in order to be held sacred, should have been actually worshipped. An object may be held sacred by a class of persons without being worshipped by them. It is clear, therefore, that the courts below were rather cynical in so lightly brushing aside the religious susceptibilities of that class of persons to which the complainant claims to belong. The section has been intended to respect the religious susceptibilities of persons of different religious persuasions or creeds. Courts have got to be very circumspect in such matters, and to pay due regard to the feelings and religious emotions of different classes of persons with different beliefs, irrespective of the consideration whether or not they share those beliefs, or whether they are rational or otherwise, in the opinion of the court."*

[Emphasis Supplied]

This Fundamental Right of Hindus is to offer due worship/ prayer at a site at Ram janmasthan in Ram janmabhoomi, where faith tells them their God was born. This right is and has been obviously an essential part of the religion and such right is and has been superior to and prevails over the ordinary legal right to property claimed by the Sunni Wakf Board as Plaintiffs in the Civil Appeals in the Hon'ble Supreme Court. The Sunni Wakf Board was only concerned with the area as a property, which is an ordinary right but even there the Shia Wakf Board, which is/was also a party in the proceedings, had conceded the claim to the Hindus to re-build the Ram Temple at the disputed site. Also, Since the alleged builder of the Babari Masjid, Mir Baqi was of the Shia sect of Islam, and his present hereditary appointee as Muthwali (a descendant of the original muthwali) of the said mosque is of the Shia Sect of Islam, hence the Shia Waqf Board was a party in proceedings therein. In fact in Islamic law the Babri Mosque belonged to the Shia denomination, because the builder Mir Baqi, as well as all the successive Muthwali were Shia and so was its present hereditary Muthwali. Both the present Shia Muthwali and the Shia Waqf Board were party to the proceedings as a party and they had declared that they are agreeable to shifting the mosque site to another location, leaving uncontested the claim of the Hindus for re-building the Ram Temple at the disputed. Critically, the Allahabad High Court had also dismissed the Sunni Wakf Board civil suit for Title to the disputed site since there is no valid notification issued under Section 5 (1) of the Muslim Wakf Act, 1936 in respect of the property in the suit. Therefore, the suit is not maintainable by the Sunni Wakf Board. Important to mention here that, in Ismail Farooqui vs Union of India [(1994) 6 SCC 360], Hon'ble Supreme Court referred to the case of Masjid Shahid Ganj v. Shiromani Gurdwara Prabandhak Committee, Amritsar [AIR 1938 Lahore 369 (FB)], wherein it was held that where a mosque has been adversely possessed by non-Muslims, it has lost its sacred character as a mosque. This order thereon was upheld by the Privy Council [AIR 1940 PC 116].

The statement of the then Prime Minister P.V. Narasimha Rao and the Central Government's commitment on 14.09.1994 filed in the Affidavit by the then Solicitor General in this Hon'ble Court, is a binding commitment presented in the Apex Court in Ismail Farooqui vs Union of India [(1994) 6 SCC 360, para 105] stating inter alia as follows:

"... If efforts at, a negotiated settlement as aforesaid do not succeed, Government is committed to enforce a solution in the light of the Supreme Court's opinion and consistent with it. Government's action in this regard will be even-handed in respect of both the communities. ***If the question referred is answered in the affirmative, namely, that a Hindu temple/structure did exist prior to the construction of the demolished structure, Government action will be in support of the wishes of the Hindu community.*** *If, on the other hand, the question is answered in the negative, namely, that no such Hindu temple/structure existed at the relevant time, then Government action will be in support of the wishes of the Muslim community."*

Subsequently there were findings in the Union Government's ASI research that there was evidence to infer that there were indicative of remains which are distinctive features found associated with the temples of north India. Excavation at the disputed site of Ram-Janmabhoomi-Babri Majid was carried out by the Archeological Survey of India (ASI) from 12 March 2003 to 7 August 2003. This excavation was carried out in pursuance of an order to get sufficient archaeological evidence on the issues involved *"whether there was any temple/structure which was demolished and mosque was constructed on the disputed site,"* the Hon'ble Lucknow Bench of the Allahabad High Court had given directions to ASI to excavate at the disputed site where the GPR Survey had suggested evidence of anomalies which could be structure, pillars, foundation walls slab flooring etc. which could be confirmed by excavation. To summaries the ASI while viewing the entire survey in toto and taking into account the archeological evidence of continuity in structural phases from the tenth century onwards up to the construction of the disputed structure along with the yield of stone and decorated bricks as well as mutilated sculpture of divine couple and carved architectural members including foliage patterns, amalaka, kapotapali doorjamb with semi-circular pilaster, broken octagonal shaft of black schist pillar, lotus motif, circular shrine having pranala (waterchute) in the north, fifty pillar bases in association of the huge structure, are indicative of remains which are distinctive features found associated with the temples of North India. [Pg 3851 of the HC judgement]. This commitment acts as a Promissory Estoppel on the State/Government since authors' and Hindu Bhakts waited without searching for any other peaceful measures within the Constitution, such as agitating for legislation enacted by Parliament for the Government through its agency, the ASI to determine on a preponderance of probability that there was indeed a pre-existing Hindu temple as per the definition in the Constitution [Article 25 (2), Explanation II].

THE ACQUISITION OF CERTAIN AREA AT AYODHYA ACT, 1993 (THE AYODHYA ACT)

The Constitutional validity of the Ayodhya Act was upheld by the judgment of this Honourable Court in Ismail Farooqui vs Union of India [(1994) 6 SCC 360], including the

Constitutional validity of Section 3[1] thereof. By virtue of the Ayodhya Act, 67.703 Acres of the "area," [as defined in the Ayodhya Act], comprising the undisputed land of Ram Janma Bhoomi/Babri Masijid stood transferred and vested in the Central Government.[2] Furthermore, 0.313 acres of land [the "disputed" land] could also had been taken over by the Government under the principle of eminent domain. Under the concept of 'eminent domain', the State has an eminent domain to take over any land.[3] Out of the area of 67.703 acres of land, the disputed area was 0.313 acres. The Central Government is only obligated to compensate the appropriate party with reasonable compensation under the Ayodhya Act. With respect to Section 7[4] of the Ayodhya Act, 1993, maintaining of the Structure is only applicable to the disputed

[1]"3. Acquisition of rights in respect of certain area. —On and from the commencement of this Act, the right, title and interest in relation to the area shall, by virtue of this Act, stand transferred to, and vest in, the Central Government."

[2]In Ismail Farooqui vs Union of India [(1994) 6 SCC 360] the Honble Supreme Court held:

"18. Broadly stated, the focus of challenge to the statute as a whole is on the grounds of secularism, right to equality and right to freedom of religion. Challenge to the acquisition of the area in excess of the disputed area is in addition on the ground that the acquisition was unnecessary being unrelated to the dispute pertaining to the small disputed area within it...."

[3]Hon'ble Supreme Court in M.Siddiq vs Mahant Suresh Das [AIR 2018 SC 5134] held:

"61.....We have already noticed that the Constitution Bench held that acquisition is a sovereign or prerogative power of the State to acquire property and all religious places, namely, church, mosque, temple etc. are liable to be acquired in exercise of right of eminent domain of the State."

[4]"7. Management of property by Government.—(1) Notwithstanding anything contained in any contract or instrument or order of any court, tribunal or other authority to the contrary, on and from the commencement of this Act, the property vested in the Central Government under section 3 shall be managed by the Central Government or by a person or body of persons or trustees of any trust authorised by that Government in this behalf.

land of 0.313 acres. The "undisputed land" [67.390 acres] therefore, by virtue of the Ayodhya Act of 1993, could had been handed back with instantaneous effect to the owners from whom the land was nationalized at the commencement of the Ayodhya Act of 1993,[5] provided they have not already accepted the Compensation given upon the nationalization of the land in 1993. Except Ram-Janmabhoomi Nyas Samathi all other Claimants had accepted the compensation and hence only the Government and the Nyas Samithi remained in the reckoning which could had been achieved harmoniously as was achieved in the case of Somnath Temple in Gujarat which was repeatedly demolished by invader Mohammed Ghazni, and which was rebuilt in the 1950's. Section 8[6] of the Ayodhya Act of 1993, further provided the procedure and mechanism for compensating the parties for the disputed area with Court's

(2) In managing the property vested in the Central Government under section 3, the Central Government or the authorised person shall ensure that the position existing before the commencement of this Act in the area on which the structure (including the premises of the inner and outer courtyards of such structure), commonly known as the Ram Janma Bhumi-Babri Masjid, stood in village Kot Ramchandra in Ayodhya, in Pargana Haveli Avadh, in tehsil Faizabad Sadar, in the district of Faizabad of the State of Uttar Pradesh is maintained.

[5]In Ismail Farooqui vs Union of India [(1994) 6 SCC 360], this Hon'ble Court observed that the undisputed land should be returned back to the original owners. Extracts of the relevant paragraph of the judgment is as follows:

"48.....This itself is a clear indication that the exercise made is to find out the true owner of the disputed area, to maintain status quo therein during the interregnum and to hand it over to the true owner found entitled to it."

[6]"8. Payment of amount.

(1) The owner of any land, building, structure or other property comprised in the area shall be given by the Central Government, for the transfer to and vesting in that Government under section 3 of that land, building, structure or other property, in cash an amount equivalent to the market value of the land, building, structure or other property.

approval. For this implementation, a "claims commissioner" was envisaged in the Ayodhya Act of 1993.Thus, under Section 8 (2) of the Ayodhya Act, 1993 the Government of India shall for the purposes of deciding the claim of the owner or any person having a claim against the owner under subsection 8(1), by notification in the official gazette, could appoint a Claims Commissioner as defined under Section 2 of the Ayodhya Act, 1993.

According to John Austin and Jeremy Bentham, *[two legal-logician's strong advocators of a society oversaw by a sovereign]* law is derived through sovereign authority, which are commands backed by sanctions for non-compliance. Building upon this, is the concept of Eminent domain enshrined in the Constitution of India implied under Article 300-A. Denotes that no-individual can outweigh ultimately the rights of the civic at large. No community should scar and raid the rights of the individual unless it be for the most imperative and vital intentions. The concept is expounded, that state can acquire any land, for a loftier public use. Provided fair, equitable and reasonable compensation is allotted to the respective party. What has to be looked into is the fairness and reasonability in

(2) The Central Government shall, for the purpose of deciding the claim of the owner or any person having a claim against the owner under sub-section (1), by notification in the Official Gazette, appoint a Claims Commissioner.

(3) The Claims Commissioner shall regulate his own procedure for receiving and deciding the claims.

(4) The owner or any person having a claim against the owner may make a claim to the Claims Commissioner within a period of ninety days from the date of commencement of this Act:

Provided that if the Claims Commissioner is satisfied that the claimant was prevented by sufficient cause from preferring the claim within the said period of ninety days, the Claims Commissioner may entertain the claim, within a further period of ninety days and not thereafter."

terms of the compensation given. The compensation has to be evenhanded and not impartial. That the Hon'ble Courts can intervene if the same fairness is not carried out or arbitrary. Applying the same concept on Eminent domain enshrined in Article 300-A of the Constitution of India, read with Article 25 and 26 was one way of solving the long-awaited dispute of Ram-Janmbhoomi/Babri Masjid dispute. By virtue of the Ayodhya Act, 67.703 Acres of the "area," [as defined in the Ayodhya Act], comprising the undisputed land of Ram Janma Bhoomi/Babri Masijid stands transferred and vested in the Central Government. Furthermore, it is submitted that a further 0.313 acres of land [the "disputed" land] can also be taken over by the Government under the concept of eminent domain. Under the concept of 'eminent domain', the State has an eminent domain to take over any land. It is most respectfully submitted that out of the area of 67.703 acres of land, the disputed area is 0.313 acres. The Central Government is obligated to compensate the appropriate party with reasonable compensation under the Ayodhya Act. In the light of Ismail Farooqui vs Union of India [(1994) 6 SCC 360] and the fact that the claim of Muslim parties is restricted only to 0.313 acres of land and the fate of the remaining undisputed area is concluded (as it is of no dispute) this undisputed area could be handed back to the original owners i.e. the Hindu parties long time back itself under Article 300-A of the Constitution of India.

To sum up, authors' reiterates, former President of India, Dr. Rajendra Prasad's statement while inaugurating the newly-constructed Somnath Temple and ceremonially re-installing the Jyotirlingam; *"Rising from its ashes again, this Temple of Somnath is to say, proclaiming to the World, that no man and no power in the World can destroy that for which the people have boundless faith and love in their hearts."* [*Source:* letter by Swami Dayananda Saraswati and others to the then (2013) Hon'ble President, Shri Pranab Mukherjee]

9 NOVEMBER 2019

On 8 November, 2019, all the primetime 9.00 PM TV news flashed the breaking news that next morning at 10.30 i.e. 9 November, the five-judge bench of the Hon'ble Supreme Court would deliver its verdict on the appeals related to Sri Ram Janma Bhumi suit. In the light of the above declaration of law, the religious sentiments of Hindus who consider the Ram Jamnabhoomi site as the birthplace of Lord Ram was respected as after 40 days of day-to-day hearing mainly on Limitation of the Suits, application of res judicata on suits, Faith and belief of Hindus which tells that Lord Ram was born at that disputed land, reliance put on the Archeological Survey of India (ASI) Report on excavation of the site, juristic person [A place being a juristic person, therefore, becoming a deity in itself] and adverse possession [Property adversely possessed by Muslims giving them the right to claim ownership of the property and enjoy continuous and uninterrupted use of the property] the most-historic monumental matter by Chief Justice Ranjan Gogoi, Justice S. A. Bobde, Justice D. Y. Chandrachud, Justice S. Abdul Nazeer and Justice Ashok Bhushan (unanimously 5:0) was inferred that the Ram-Janmabhoomi (The Disputed Site) on the root of faith and belief of the Hindus is not unsubstantiated. The existence prior to 1528 AD, can be traced and corroborated through vast scriptures and sacred religious books including Valmiki Ramayana and Skanda Purana. To pave the way for the ultimate determination of the relief to be granted in para 788 the Hon'ble Supreme Court summarized and explains the position of the Archeological Survey of India (ASI) conducted in 2003. Hon'ble Court inferred the position as follows:

(*a*) The excavation by the ASI has revealed the existence of a preexisting underlying structure dating back to the twelfth century. The structure has large dimensions, evident from the fact that there were 85 pillar bases comprised in 17 rows each of five pillar bases.

(*b*) On a preponderance of probabilities, the archaeological findings on the nature of the underlying structure indicate it to be of Hindu religious origin, dating to twelfth century A.D.

(*c*) The mosque in dispute was constructed upon the foundation of the pre-existing structure. The construction of the mosque has taken place in such a manner as to obviate an independent foundation by utilizing the walls of the pre-existing structure;

(*d*) The layered excavation at the site of excavation has also revealed the existence of a circular shrine together with a makara pranala indicative of Hindu worship dating back to the eighth to tenth century.

Further, standard of proof governing civil trial was inferred on the basis of the ASI report. The inference was made-out that the foundation of mosque is based on the walls of a large pre-existing structure which locates back to twelfth century. Importantly, the underlying structure were suggestive of a Hindu religious origin comparable to temple excavations in the region, tracing of that epoch. However, the Hon'ble Court also read and found that the Report did not provide the reason for the destruction of the Pre-existing structure and the pre-determined motive and/or purpose to demolish Temple was to construct mosque. The Hon'ble Curt further found a time-gap between the date of the underlying structure and the construction of the mosque, inferring that there was no-evidence as to explain the course of time gap between the underlying structure and the construction of the mosque of four centuries. Therefore, Hon'ble Court's finding of the title was not solely based on the archaeological findings.

Further, the Court also chronicled certain historical travelers record indicating the existence of the faith and belief of the Hindus that the disputed site was the birth-place of Lord Ram and discernable places of offering devotion by the Hindus comprising Sita Rasoi, the bedi (cradle) and Swargdwar epitomizing the birth of Lord Ram in and around the disputed site. The travelers integrated mainly Tieffenthaler and the interpretation of Montgomery Martin of the eighteenth century. The Hon'ble Court, did not fully rely on the observations of the travelers mentioned above, while noting that such accounts must be read with circumspection. Not merely relying on faith or belief, but at the same time respecting the same, Hon'ble Court notes that Faith and belief are indicators towards patterns of worship at the site on the basis of which claim of position are asserted.

The Apex Court also, notes that the erection of structure of Islamic oppression in Ayodhya, failed to shake the faith and belief of Hindus that Lord Ram was born at the disputed Site. The existence of such structure, did not stop Hindus from enduring their worship at the disputed site and within the precincts of the edifice former to the confrontations of 1856-1857. Decisively, the Hon'ble Court noted that open, exclusive and unhindered possession of the outer courtyard including worship at Ram Chabutra, Sita Rasoi and at other religious places and setting up of a Bhandar was enjoyed by Hindu Worshipers. Further, the Muslims were not in the possession of the outer courtyard. Also, noting the erection of the wall in 1858 by the British and the setting up of the Ram Chabutra in close-propinquity of the inner-dome, Hindu worshipers continued to avow their right to pray inside the three-domed configuration. That the Authors claimed the same Right pray at the disputed site enshrined in the Constitution of India read with the preamble forming the basic structure of the Constitution of India. Noting the testimonies of both Hindu and Muslim witnesses, the Court noted that the same reveals that on religious junctures and festivals like Ram Navmi, Kartik Poornima, Parikrama Mela and Ram Vivah, Hindu devotees and worshipers in large congregations visited the disputed premises for dharshan. Further, the pattern of Worship and prayer towards the Grab Grih can be located through the oral testimony of the Hindu Devotes. Additionally, Muslim witnesses have acknowledged the presence of symbols of Hindu religious significance both inside and outside the mosque.

Subsequently, Hon'ble Court decided from the emerging evidentiary record that the disputed site is one composite whole. The railing set-up in 1856-7 did not either bring about a sub-division of the land or any determination of title. Plaintiff of Suit No. 4, the Sunni Waqf Board failed to establish its case of a dedication by user. Furthermore, the alternate plea of adverse possession has not been established by the plaintiffs of Suit no. 4, as they have failed to meet the requirements of adverse possession. Importantly, the Hindus were in exclusive and unimpeded possession of the outer courtyard where they have continued worship. The Hon'ble Court further summaries that the impairment to the mosque in 1934, its discretion in 1949 leading to the ouster of the Muslims and the eventual obliteration on 6 December 1992 comprised a serious disruption of the Rule of Law. At this juncture the Court establishes that the possessory title to the outside courtyard by virtue of long, continued and unimpeded worship at the Ram Chabutra and other objects of religious significance is of clear case of Hindus. Further, the possession of the three-domed structure in the inner courtyard was contested by the Muslims and Hindus. The assertion by the Hindus of entitlement to offer worship enriched in the Preamble and in the Article 25 of the Constitution of India was contested by the Muslims. With respect to the inner courtyard, the Hon'ble Court analyzed that there is evidence on a preponderance of probabilities to establish worship by the Hindus prior to the annexation of Oudh by the British in 1857, on the other hand Muslims failed to offer any evidence to indicate that they were in exclusive possession of the inner structure prior to 1857 since the erection in the sixteenth century. Ultimately, annulling the impugned order of the High Court of Allahabad (2010) i.e. of allocating 2/3rd to the Hindu parties and 1/3rd to the Muslim Party, Hon'ble Supreme Court held that the treatment of the disputed land/composite land will be done as a whole and not sub-division of the title. The Apex Court held that the High Court erred in granting relief to the party(s), not treating land as one composite land and sub-dividing it. The Hon'ble Court held that the three-way bifurcation by the High Court was legally unsustainable. Diving the land would not sub-serve the interest of either of the parties or secure a lasing sense of peace and tranquility.

In conclusion, the Hon'ble Supreme Court held Suit 5 held to be maintainable at the behest of the first plaintiff, Ram Lalla

Virajman (the deity of Lord Ram) who is a juristic person. Subsequently, partly decreed Suit 4 (Plaintiff: the Sunni Central Waqf Board) by directing the allotment of alternate land to the Muslims for construction of a mosque and associated activities. The Apex Court felt the need and necessity to allot the alternate land to the Muslims because though on a balance of probabilities. Furthermore, the Apex Court held that apart from the disputed property and Muslim Party(s) not having any rights over the composite land; it was indispensable to provide for a restitution to the community for the unlawful destruction of their place of worship on 6 December 1992. For this purpose and considering the heavy weighted nature of the relief, the Court directed that land admeasuring 5 acres be allotted to the Sunni Central Waqf Board [Plaintiff Suit no. 4] either by the Central Government out of the acquired land or by the Government of Uttar Pradesh within the city of Ayodhya. Earlier argued, the Government is/was fully entrusted with power under eminent domain to acquire the land and compensate. The Hon'ble Court under Article 142 of the Constitution of India, also directed the Union Government, to formulate a scheme with respect to the powers enshrined in the Acquisition of Certain Area at Ayodhya Act 1993, Section 6 and 7 to set-up a trust with a board of trustees or of any other appropriate body as described under section 6 of the Act of 1993. The purpose is to provide essential provisions in regard to operations of the trust or body embracing on matters concerning to the management of the trust, the powers of the trustees including the construction of a temple and all necessary, incidental and supplemental matters. Also, critical to mention that the stipulated time-frame penned by the Court on 9 November 2019 was of 3 months from the said date of pronouncement.

The precise role enriched in the Constitution of India under Article 31A (1)(b) of limited time frame of Governments role in taking over of the management is also reflected in the Judgment. That Possession of the inner and outer courtyards shall be handed over to the Board of Trustees of the Trust or to the body so constituted while before, handing over to the Trust, as an acting period possession of the disputed property shall continue to vest in the statutory receiver under the Central Government. Hon'ble Court held Suit 3 filed by Nirmohi Akhara barred by limitation and rejected the objection of the petitioners and of Sunni Waqf Board to maintainability of Suit no. 5, which was Nirmohi Akhara's claim to be a shebait. The instant claim was rejected by the Hon'ble Court. However, the Apex Court to take recourse to its power under Article 142 to do complete justice, directed that in framing of the scheme, an appropriate role in the management would be assigned to the plaintiffs of Suit no. 3. The rights of the Plaintiff in Suit no. 1 to worship at the Disputed property.

Finally, based on facts, oral evidence(s), oral presentations, religious sacred texts and scripts which navigated history, law, faith and belief of Hindus prior to 1528 A.D, was relied on by the Hon'ble Court to conjecture that possession of inner and outer courtyard shall be handed over to the Board of trustees of the Trust or the Body so constituted; while Union Government shall make suitable provisions in respect of the rest of the acquired land by handling it over to the trust or body for development and management in terms of the scheme framed.

ADDENDUM

The addenda produced after the Judgment, traces period prior to the period of 1528 A.D. The Addenda locates, that the religious faith of a person is formed on traditions, religious scriptures and practices. While, recognizing the stature and importance of Religious scriptures as the main source of Hinduism being the foundations on the basis on which faith of Hindus is established and honored. Further, sheds light on the historical assessment and value of Valmiki Ramayan as the main-spring of understanding of Lord Ram and his actions. The existence of Valmiki's Ramayan is traced back to the period of Before Christ (B.C.) and also before the period of Mahabhart and Shrimad Bhagwad Gita. For this purpose, the author of Addendum is relying on the statement of witness (PW-18), Suvira Jaiswal, a historian. In the statement of witness, she states that "the period of Valmiki Ramayan is recorded as 300 B.C. – 200 B.C.." Further, the Addenda locates the importance of the birth place of Lord Ram, which is refereed in the Valmiki Ramayan. The manuscript associates the Birth of Lord Ram with Ayodhya in Balakhand, Canto XVIII Shlok 8 to 12 with planter situations. Further, Shlok 10 elucidates on the birth of Lord Ram as son of Kaushalya at Ayodhya. Another religious inscription relied upon, is the Skand Puran. There are various illustrations and Sholaks where the place/location of Ram Janmabhoomi/Ram Janmasthan is mentioned in the Puran. The addendum, concluding on the Sanskrit inscriptions, scared religious books including Valmiki Ramayan and Skand Puran held that the faith and belief of Hindus regarding location of birth place of Lord Ram cannot be held to be unsubstantiated. Further, found that there are enough and sufficient religious texts in the period prior to 1528 A.D., leading to Author(s) belief and faith enshrined in the basic structure of the Constitution of India that the present Site of Ram Janmbhoomi as the Birthplace of Lord Ram. Subsequent to the period of 1528 A.D. and before 31.10.1858, the addenda traces' the existence of "Shri Ramcharitmanas" of Goswami Tulsidas [i.e. composed in 1574-75 A.D.] It is well-established and well-honored, the distinctive place of the instant Epic and like the Valmiki Ramayan, which further launches the status of Hindu faith and belief. The Chaupaiyas comments on Lord Vishnu taking Human-form in Ayodhya and decidedly mentions human-form at the House of King Dasaratha and Kausalya. Moreover, reference of another book was filed as an exhibit. The book called "Hadith-e-Sehba" written in the year 1856 by, Mirza Jaan. The said book mentions that the place of worship called as Birthplace of Lord Ram which is adjacent to "Sita-Ki-Rasoi," and the mosque was erected by Babar. Therefore, the book unequivocally consents to the Janmasthan of Lord Ram and subsequent to erection of Mosque by Babar. Faith and Belief of Hindus with respect to the Ram Janmasthaan during the period 1858 to 1949 can be traced and documented through several Gazetteers, reports of ASI, books and other documentary evidence which was exhibited in the suits. Critical to mention that the British Government took control over the Area w.e.f 01.11.1858, and in all form of documentation, corresponding and/or orders issued, the mosque was always referred to as "Mosque Janmasthan." Implying that the British Officials also always treated the Mosque as the Janmasthan of Lord Ram. Further, Historical Sketches of Tehsil Fyzabad prepared by P. Carnegy [Overseeing Commissioner and settlement officer of Ayodhya and Fyzabad] and published by the Government in 1870 shapes that Ayodhya is to Hindus what Mecca is to the Mohammadan and Jerusalem to the Jews. Further, categorizes and refers the Janmasthan as the place of birth of Lord Ram, where Babar built a mosque in his name in A.D. 1528. Secondly, noticing the Report of ASI of North West Provinces and Oudh dated 1889 which stated that "the Old Temple of Ramchandra at Janmasthan must have been a very fine one, for many of its columns have been used by the Musalmans in the construction of Babars Masjid." Substantiated by two more ASI Report(s); it is clear that Babar's Masjid at ayodhya was built on the very spot where the Temple Janmasthan of Lord Ram was standing. Subsequently, many applications were filed before Sub-Judge Faizabad in 1885-86 to sought permission to re-built Ram Temple at the disputed spot. Many applications filed refer Babri Mosque as Janmasthan Masjid locating the significance and indicating that the Mosque was situated at the Janmasthan of Lord Ram. Further the aforementioned was corroborated on many examinations of oral evidence of witnesses of Plaintiff Suit No. 5, 3 and 4. According to the addendum, the said oral evidences and statements lucidly demonstrates faith and belief of Hindus that Janmasthan of Lord Ram is the habitation where Babri Mosque has been fabricated. The oral evidence in the Civil Suits proves, the status of the Three-domed structure as the Birth Place of Lord Ram, Parikrama of the entire premises by the Devotees.

Building upon the sequence of events and to sum up, the Faith and Belief of Hindus signposts that the disputed land was the place of birth of Lord Ram i.e. the three-dome structure mosque which was erected and fabricated at the Janmasthan. It is further noted that, it was the British Government in 1856-7, instituting the iron wall bi-furcating the outer courtyard and inner courtyard to keep Hindus outside the grilled iron wall in the Outer Courtyard. It was subsequent of the construction of the wall, Worship and Puja started in Ram Chabutra in the outer courtyard. Additionally, Suit in 1885 was filed seeking authorization to paradigm temple on the said land where worship was permitted by the British Government. Based on various evidence on record, depicting faith and belief of the Hinds clearly establishes that the mosque was constructed at the place of birth of Lord Ram and the three-dome structure is the Janmasthan of Lord Ram. Critically, the faith and belief of Hindus cannot be altered regarding the Birth Place of Lord Ram, on the mere fact that the Hindus were contracting iron-wall, diving Mosque premises, keeping outside the three-dome edifice. The sole worship on the Ram Chabutra, as inferred by the Hon'ble Court in the addendum is that in the Outer Courtyard, worship was symbolic of Lord Ram, believed according to Hindus to be born in the said premises. Ultimately, the Apex Court on 9 November, 2019 in the addendum concluded in Paragraph 170 "*...on the conclusion that faith and belief of Hindus was prior to the construction of the Mosque and subsequent thereto has always been that*

Janmasthan of Lord Ram is the place where Babri Mosque has been constructed which faith and belief is proved by documentary and oral evidence."

That the Authors assessment are that the Hon'ble Court being vigilant about the Situation and careful in not favoring any one sect / denomination/ religion, has based the judgment on evidence. But it is critical to analyze that the said evidence is based on the Faith, belief and Worship of the devotees, plaintiffs and Witnesses and the authors. The same Faith, belief and worship which has to be secured and enshrined in the Constitution of India. The faith and belief enshrined in the Preamble read with Article 25 and 26 of the Constitution of India, having a superseding nature and status when compared to an ordinary right of property had to prevail. Also, Faith and belief of Hindus elucidating that the Disputed Site was the birthplace of Ram was further substantiated in various Epics and Judicial pronouncements. All the evidence indicated that there was continuum of faith and belief of the Hindus that the 'Garbh-Grih' was the place of birth of Lord Ram. The process of drawing inferences from data was an essential element of archaeology as a discipline but to reject this exercise as conjectural and hypothetical would be a dis-service both to the discipline and to the underlying process. Archaeological finds in the area of excavation reveal significant traces of successive civilizations, commencing with the age of the North Black Polished Ware traceable to the second century B.C., (i.e., older than 2200 years). The faith and belief of the Hindus is that Lord Ram was born inside the inner sanctum or 'Garbh Grih' right below the central dome of the three-domed structure the faith and belief of the Hindus that Lord Ram was born in Ayodhya is/was undisputed. In furtherance, Muslim witnesses also stated that Hindus have faith and belief in the existence of the Janmasthan. The wall dividing the outer and the inner courtyard was built in 1857 CE and the worship of Hindus in the outer courtyard continued always unimpeded. As regards the inner courtyard, there was evidence to establish worship by the Hindus prior to the annexation of Oudh by the British in 1857. Additionally, the

Muslims have offered no evidence to indicate that they were in exclusive possession of the inner structure prior to 1857 since the date of the construction in the sixteenth century (1528 CE).The Hon'ble Court did not entertain claims that stem from the actions of the Mughal rulers against Hindu places of worship in a Court of law today. Thus, while Suit-1 (filed by Gopal Singh Visharad in 1950 CE) and Suit-5 (filed on behalf of Bhagwan Ramlala Virajman in 1989) have been held to be decreed in full, Suit-4 (filed by Sunni Central Waqf Board in 1961) has been partly decreed and Suit-3 (filed by Nirmohi Akhara in 1959) has been held to be dismissed being barred by Limitation.The significance of Mosque(s) and temple was interpreted by various Hon'ble Court(s), which was relied upon to come to such conclusion. Sanatam Dharma prevailed. Justice prevailed. Oldest land-faith dispute was resolved subsequently.

REVIEW

After retirement of Hon'ble Chief Justice Ranjan Gogoi, the new 5-Judge Bench compromising of the new Chief Justice S. A. Bobde, Justice D. Y. Chandrachud, Justice S. Abdul Nazeer, Justice Ashok Bhushan and Justice Sanjiv Khanna took 18 review petitions seeking re-assessment of Hon'ble Court's November 9 judgement, however ultimately resulted in closing of the doors on any further review. The Hon'ble Bench rejected all 18 review petitions in-chamber. Set of 9 filings was sought by parties who were part of the earlier litigation and oddly, the other nine were filed by "third parties." The only legal Couse left now is when a petitioner points out a legal error(s) in the 9 November judgment to seek review i.e. Curative Review petition.

The first review petition seeking review of Ayodhya verdict was filed on 2 December, 2019 by Maulana Syed Ashhad Rashidi [Uttar Pradesh President, Jamiat Ulama-e-Hind], legal heir of original litigant M Siddiq. Sought review of the verdict on 14 counts and said that "complete justice" could only be done by directing reconstruction of Babri Masjid. He also sought an interim stay on operation of the verdict in which it had directed the Centre that a trust be formed within three months for construction of the temple at the site. Subsequently, on 6 December, six petitions other reviewpetitions were filed in the apex court seeking review of its November 9 judgement. Additionally, on 9 December, Akhil Bharat Hindu Mahasabha filed another review petition seeking review of the Verdict. Though, the pray was limited with respect to review on direction to allot a five-acre plot to Sunni Waqf Board for building a mosque in Ayodhya. On 9 December another review petition was filed by 40 rights activists.

CHAPTER 4

Sanskrit as National Link Language

In India's long continuous history, Sanskrit has been the greatest integrating force, the source of cultural continuum, the medium of literary creativity, the voice of the sages and the language of the most sublime thoughts and the profoundest of the philosophies of life. It was the medium of intellectual and spiritual discourse and made its impact on scholars throughout the length and breadth of the country. A Virat Hindu needs to learn Sanskrit to have this access to this vast ocean of knowledge. In the centuries to come, it is Sanskrit that will be the most sensible link language for us Indians. There are two reasons for it. The first is that all Indian languages have a high proportion of words taken from Sanskrit. In the case of Bengali and Malayalam it may be 90 per cent, while in the case of Tamil it is at least 42 per cent (even in the DMK version of "pure" Tamil). Bengali is proudly referred to as the "daughter" of Sanskrit, but Tamil which has a proud history of its own, thanks to the long unbroken reign of the Chola kingdoms, is accepted by Sanskrit scholars as the "sister" of Sanskrit.

For this reason, Sanskritized Hindi is easier to understand for the Southerners (and difficult for those Northerners like Nehru steeped in Urdu). The late Annadurai of DMK used to say that for Sanskritized Hindi, "naa vadiyar" (I am teacher). Incidentally, the Tamil word "vadiyar" is a respectable way to address from the Sanskrit word "vadi" (preacher). For this reason of common vocabulary, Sanskrit is ultimately the best national link language for India.

Secondly, international research in today's most advanced area of computers, namely, Artificial Intelligence, which is to revolutionize the knowledge systems of the 21st Century, is now increasingly coming to the conclusion that Sanskrit is the best language to store knowledge in a computer. Dr. Rick Briggs of the US National Aeronautics and Space Agency (NASA), in an article titled "Knowledge Representation in Sanskrit and Artificial Intelligence" that:

> "In the past twenty years, much time, effort, money has been expended on designing an unambiguous representation of natural languages to make them accessible to computer processing. Understandably, there is widespread belief that natural languages are unsuitable for the transmission of many ideas that artificial languages can render with great precision and mathematical rigour. There is at least one language, Sanskrit ... (in which) can be reckoned a method ... that is identical not only in essence but in form with current work in Artificial Intelligence."

This article demonstrates that a natural language (Sanskrit) can serve as an artificial language also, and that much work in Artificial Intelligence has been reinventing a wheel millennium old." The grammarian—Panini—is now being called the first software man, without the hardware. And the focus is on the roughly 4,000 rules of Sanskrit grammar that the evolved. Rules that are so scientific and logical in manner that they closely resemble structures used by computer scientists throughout the world. Since Sanskrit is said to be the mother of most Indian languages [Tamil being a sister of Sanskrit], scientists are trying to develop a mathematical and computational grammar for them. These are "catchy ideas" in artificial intelligence today, with pioneering work now being done in India, US and Germany. Interestingly, many scientists are tempted to speculate how Panini developed his rules in so concise and precise a manner without a computer in 3995 aphorisms in his *Ashtadhyayi.*

Thus, as we look back, it seems that the founding fathers of the Independence Movement committed a blunder in not inserting Sanskrit its rightful place. Sanskrit is an essential component of the substance of Indian Asmita. What came out of all that discussion in the Constituent Assembly was that subsequently, Sanskrit was included in the 8th Schedule of the Constitution as one of the Indian languages (the number of these languages has now gone up to 18). Also, it was provided that Hindi, which was to the endorsed language and written in Sanskrit's Devanagari script [Article 340 of the Constitution], would be developed by drawing wherever necessary for its vocabulary primarily on Sanskrit [Article 351].

This was a "holding operation" compromise for make it a link language. Nehru himself continued to pretend reverence for Sanskrit. While speaking in Parliament on a Private Member's Bill in 1959, Nehru *inter alia* said that people grew from their roots. India had a history of 5,000 to 10,000 years. Language was a symbol of continuity. The language to which most Indian languages were connected was Sanskrit, but it was lip service. In reality Nehru sabotaged the cause of Sanskrit. He made a mockery of All India Radio Hindi broadcasts as being "incomprehensible" to him. Sanskrit has made the most significant contribution to the development of all the Indian languages. With the exception of four languages of the South, almost all the major Indian languages had their source and derived their sustenance from Sanskrit. The languages of the South also had a large part of their vocabulary derived from Sanskrit. Anti-Hindi zealots today confuse Devanagiri with Hindi. The truth is that Hindi is just one of the languages using this script of Sanskrit. Marathi, Sindhi, and some of the Hill tract languages additionally use Devanagiri. This script thus can be used by any language. In fact, the scripts of all Indian languages even including Tamil and *Devanagiri* [considered as "sisters"] are direct descendants of the original *Brahmi* script. Any competent linguist would tell you that. The *Gurumukhi* script is very similar to the *Devanagiri* script, just as the Gujarati script is. Anyone who knows *Devanagiri* can master Gurumukhi in 24 hours. Yet a senseless agitation took place to oppose Gurumukhi in Punjab, followed by an unhealthy polarization process that culminated in Operation Bluestar in 1984, the tragic after-effects of which, we feel even today.

In a calm dispassionate atmosphere which may take decades to attain, young people, especially those entering primary and secondary schools, should be made to learn at least two languages and two scripts: (1) mother tongue and Sanskrit and (2) own script and Devanagiri. In the meantime, Hindi should continue to Sanskritize itself to the point where it becomes almost indistinguishable from Sanskrit. It will then merge into Sanskrit, thereby disappearing except in local dialects. Sanskrit was once long ago uprooted from India by Pali. But after some centuries, this versatile language was rethroned by the same process via *Mahayana* Buddhism and by Sanskritising the vocabulary of Pali. A second rethroning of Sanskrit can now be achieved through Sanskritising Hindi. Till that day, the three languages formula, which requires northerners to learn one southern language, if sincerely implemented, we can make a steady progress towards the goal of re-throning Sanskrit once again the national link language of Bharat. The direction in which Nehru steered the nation during the seventeen years as Prime Minister was towards continued imitation of the culture of the European, and develop the economy on the Soviet Communist model. This has today caused an identity crisis in the youth. Since the world view of economic development has now completely changed. It is no more thought of as capital-driven or as labour driven as Karl Marx had argued, but as largely knowledge-driven. For application of knowledge, we need innovations, which means more original research and in turn which needs more-fresh young minds—the cream of the youth—to be imbibed with appropriate learning, emotional drive and striving at the frontiers of research.

This requires adequate empowerment of mental faculty endowed with multi-dimensional intelligence. It is not adequate merely to foster *cognitive* intelligence only, as universities are doing today. The message of the Bhagwat Gita is that there are other dimensions of intelligences, and recognized now abroad as *emotional,social, moral, spiritual, environmental* and *innovational*. Our vast youth population is our demographic potential dividend, that can be tapped for national regeneration only if equipped and enabled with the seven multi-dimensional intelligence. For decades since Independence in 1947 we had been told that India's demography was the main liability, that India's population was growing too fast, and what India needed most was to control its population, even if by coercive methods.

Author had challenged this view as long ago as 1972, arguing that population growth was not India's problem [Noted demographer, Dr. Ashish Bose of the University of Delhi had published in 1972 my research as a chapter in his book titled: *India's Population*, in which I had argued that the youth of India would if empowered with education be an asset to the country's development and not a liability]. Author argued then that modern science, and through the scientific innovations of freshly educated research minded youngsters, can overcome the limitations of land, natural resources and production. Author had then also called coercive family planning as "an obsession of developed nations." But the negative view of population prevailed till the 'nasbandi' [vasectomy] fiasco of the Emergency in 1975-77, which forced Indian politicians to become less vocal about the need for coercive family planning. But the prejudice about population growth in India continues into the 21st century.

Globally, India today leads in the supply of youth, i.e., persons in the age group of 15 to 35 years, and this lead will last for another forty years. We should not therefore squander this "natural resource." We must, by proper policy for the young, realize and harvest this demographic potential. China is the second largest world leader in young population today. But the youth population in that country will start shrinking in proportion of total population from 2015, i.e., less than a decade from now because of lagged negative effect of their coercive one-child policy. Japanese and European total populations are already fast aging due to economic factors, and will start declining in absolute numbers from this year (2009). The US will however hold a steady trend thanks to a liberal policy of immigration, especially from Mexico and Philippines. But even then, the US will have a demographic shortage in skilled personnel. All developed countries will experience a demographic deficit. India on the other hand will have a demographic dividend for most of the 21st century if we empower our youth with multiple intelligences. Our past liability, thus by a fortuitous turn of fate, has now become our potential asset for the future.

Thus, India has now become, by unintended consequences, gifted with a young population. If we educate this youth to develop cognitive intelligence to become original thinkers, imbibe emotional intelligence to have team spirit and rational risk—taking attitude, inculcate moral intelligence to blend personal ambition with national goals, and cultivate social intelligence to defend civic rights of the weak, gender equality, the courage to fight injustice, the spiritual intelligence to tap into the cosmic energy that surrounds the earth, the environment intelligence to preserve the integrity of Nature, and innovational intelligence to transcend limitations of resources, then we can develop a superior mindset of the Indian youth who can be relied on to contribute to make India a global power within two decades.

The concept of identity for an Indian is imperative for a nation in order to respond to challenges to its independence, culture and moral fabric. A nation must be of citizens with high level of integrity and patriotism. Integrity implies the inner strength and equilibrium which enables one to meet with equanimity the victories and set backs of contemporary politics. All who have been in public life know of those moments when the problems surrounding them appeared insurmountable, and their means to deal with them grossly inadequate. There are times when darkness gathers such as during the Emergency (1975-77), and one despairs whether the dawn will ever break out. It is at such times that one has to call upon those inner reserves of strength and power with which every human being is potentially equipped but which requires a spiritual evolution to realize. Such persons are called "Virat." Not everyone can be like that. But those who evolve to be so become time tested leaders of the nation and inspire the people to strive harder and sacrifice narrow self-interests for the larger good of the nation. Hindutva or Hinduness thus envisages a collective mindset that identifies India as the motherland from the Himalayas to the Indian Ocean and with it's glorious past. However pious a Hindu is, however prosperous Hindu temples become from doting devotees' offerings, *it is this collective mindset of the people that matters,* and not the piety of the individual alone in that collective. For that it is suggested that the religious minorities can join in if they are proud of the truth that they are descendants of Hindus. Then our nation may be defined as Hindustan i.e., a land of Hindus and those others who proudly acknowledge that their ancestors are Hindus. There are therefore eight components of the Hindutva induced mindset that the nation needs today:

First, India's Hindus and others must regard and foster the concept of the nation as the unbroken civilization of Hindustan; and their common history of endeavors, struggles, defeats and victories. Ancient Hindus and their descendants have always lived in this area from the Himalayas to the Indian Ocean an area called Akhand Hindustan, and did not come from outside.

Second, Hindutva requires that national policies for development should synchronize and harmonize material goals with spiritual advancement, which is Deendayal Upodhyaya's Integral Humanism philosophy.

Third, Modern India is a Spiritual State that adopts the concept: *sarva pantha sama bhaava.* Hence the declaration in the

Preamble of the Constitution that India is a Secular State should be replaced by that of a Spiritual State.

Fourth, a national law requiring prohibition of induced and collective religious conversion. Such a law will however not bar re-conversion to Hindu religion, or the return of any Indian to his or her ancestor's faith.

Fifth, that there is no theologically sanctioned concept of birth based social hierarchy. Varna never was conceived as birth-based in Hindu scriptures, but a choice that was subject to each abiding by the prescribed disciplines of that Varna. The present practice of birth-determined Varna is un-Hindu, and is excess baggage to be off-loaded and purged from the body-politic of the nation is the interest of a virat Hindu unity.

Sixth, all Hindus to qualify as true Hindus must make effort to learn Sanskrit and the Devanagari script, in addition to mother tongue, and pledge that one day in the future, Sanskrit will evolve to become India's link language since all the main Indian languages already have a large percentage of their vocabulary derived from or in common with Sanskrit. To re-throne Sanskrit, Hindi, vocabulary should keep Sanskritising Hindi itself becomes indistinguishable from Sanskrit, just as Pali became two thousand years ago.

Seventh, Hindus must prefer to lose everything they possess rather than submit to tyranny or to terrorism.

Eighth, the Hindutva art of governance would be structured on the principles of Ramrajya and the tenets Arthsastra of Chanakya the Hindu must have a mindset to retaliate when attacked. The retaliation must be massive enough to deter future attacks.

These eight attributes constitute a mindset that a modern Hindu must have to be in a position to confront the challenge that Hindu civilization is facing from Islamic terrorists and from fraud foreign Christian missionaries, who unfortunately are also aided and abetted from within the country by confused Hindus. Without such a virile mindset which is Virat Hindutva, Hindus will be unable to confront the subversion and erosion that today undermine the Hindu foundation of India. This foundation is what makes India distinctive, and hence we must safeguard it with all the might and moral fiber that we have. National renaissance flows out from that. India today culturally is a Hindu dominant nation, albeit politically a secular Republic. But still, in the Articles of the Constitution, the Hindu cultural primacy, i.e., Hindutva is recognized. The Hindutva flavour emerges in various Constitutional institutions such as Parliament, Supreme Court, etc, which have Sanskrit slokas as their motto, such as Satyameva Jayate, Dharma Chakra Pravartana etc.

The Official language Hindi has to be written in the Sanskrit script of Devanagari [Article 343], and where necessary, Hindi must augment its vocabulary primarily from Sanskrit language [Article 351]. Although it was a Constitutional mandate that while secularism and equality before law are a part of our core values, nevertheless the flavour and primacy for social and economic development of the nation is rooted in Hindu values. This becomes clear in the Directive Principles of State Policy [Articles 38 to 51 and 51 A]. In the governance of the country these directive principles have to be followed, and it shall be the duty of the State to apply these principles while making laws [Article 37]. What are these Directive Principles based on Hindu values? Gender equality is ensured in education, employment, wages, and inheritance [Article 39], Panchayat system for village administration [Article 40], Uniform Civil

Code [Article 44], Prohibition of liquor consumption [Article 47], Ban on slaughter of cows [Article 48], and Preservation of our rich heritage of our composite culture [Article 51A(f)]. It is obvious that these principles are all rooted in Hindu culture and constitutionally are the guiding directives for enacting laws.

Hindu theology also extols transparency and accountability due to the concepts of *satyam, shivam and sundaram,* and in the concept of *karma* which is nothing but a concept of accountability. The concept of *yama* and *niyama* define the code for Hindus, and constitute an ingredient of Hindutva. The concept of our modern nation, thus, is rooted in our ancient Hindu heritage. India is a new Republic but also an ancient Hindu nation. Hindu civilization is the longest surviving, unbroken, continuing, and unique ancient culture. The Constitution of a nation is the framework of principles, values, and canons on which the society's governance is rooted. It is either codified as a written document as in India and US, or unwritten and based on precedents as in UK.

From the Constitution flow the criminal and civil statutes which lay down the laws which the citizen has to obey, and the failure to do so invites sanctions and punishments that include imprisonment and/or penalties such as a fine. Enforcement of these statutes is the Rule of Law. India is, according to the Constitution, a Union of States not a Federation of Provinces. Hence no state can secede from the Union, and no territory however small can be amputated out of India henceforth. States can be temporarily or partly administered by the Centre.

Thus, Article 356 of the Constitution allows the Centre to take over the administration of any State for a temporary period. Articles 247 to 253 empower Parliament to enact laws and establish courts to enable the central Executive to supersede the state's Executive in administering law and order. There is a central civil service and a central police force positioned in the states. Thus, the essence or quality of the modern Indian Constitution is unitary. We must safeguard this quality for our national integrity. In our Constitution, the Hon'ble Supreme Court of India has perhaps a wider jurisdiction than the highest court in any other Constitution. That is, while citizen rights are defined by the Constitution, it is to be enforced and given content by the judiciary. The judiciary is neither subservient to the Government on the one hand nor to the people on the other. The judiciary therefore stands above the popular frenzy and the Government might. As Parliament and Legislatures represent the Will of the sovereign people, the judiciary must represent the conscience of the sovereign people. One is secured by periodical elections, while the other is ensured by life-long training, character, and experience. These two uphold the constitutionality in the rule of law. In order that the spirit of justice may prevail in the society, therefore a well-defined Constitution and independent minded judges are as essential as the structure of Institutions, so that laws are understood and well-administered. Strong, impartial and capable judiciary is the greatest need of the hour today as we are passing through testing times globally. The Constitution is a framework of rights and duties for the citizens. Basic human rights are fundamental rights, but these are not absolute, being subject to reasonable restrictions.

For example, the fundamental right of free speech and expression enshrined in Article 19(1)(a), is contrary to popular view, subject to reasonable restrictions prescribed by Article 19(2). Constitution thus recognizes no right as absolute. The Hon'ble Supreme Court has laid down the test and scope of "reasonableness" in a catena of judgments [e.g., in (1998) 8 SCC 227 para 13 page 233]. For instance, to be a reasonable restriction, it cannot conflict with Article 51(c) of the Constitution under the Directive Principles of State Policy.

The scope of the fundamental right can thus be circumscribed by law passed by Parliament. Lack of understanding of this causes ideologues such of Marxism-Leninism, popularly known is Naxalism, which advocate secession, or to fanatic religious hate group leaders such as those propagating Jehadi Islam justify evil and violent practices against non-believers. The concept of Fundamental Rights {Part III of the Indian Constitution} was not a legacy of allegedly 'humane' British Colonial legacy, as British historians claim. The demand for constitutional guarantees of human rights by Indians was made as far back as in 1895 in the Constitution of India Bill, popularly called the Swaraj Bill, which was inspired by Lokmanya Tilak, one of the great freedom fighters and architects of India's independence. This Bill envisaged for India a Constitution guaranteeing to every one of its citizens freedom of expression, inviolability of one's house, right to property, equality before the law, equal opportunity of admission to public offices, right to present claims, petitions and complaints and right to personal liberty. This the British rejected. In the Madras Session of the Indian National Congress in 1927 it was laid down that the basis of a future Constitution must be a declaration of fundamental rights. But the British Government's Simon Commission in 1930 turned down the demand for fundamental rights on the ground that "abstract declarations are useless, unless there exist the will and the means to make them effective." So much for the British claim of the legacy left behind by them. In 1952, the

Supreme Court held that fundamental rights were within the power of amendment granted under Article 368 of the Constitution. In 1965, though the question did not directly arise, the Supreme Court by a majority of three to two *reaffirmed* the view that the amending power could reach fundamental rights. Strong doubts were however expressed by two Judges, namely, Mr. Justice Hidayatullah and Mr. Justice Mudholkar about the amendability of fundamental rights. But in 1967, the Supreme Court in the Goraknath case, by a thin majority of six to five reversed their earlier two rulings, and held that Parliament had *no power* to amend any of the provisions of Part III of the Constitution so as to take away or abridge fundamental right {AIR 1967 SC 1641}.

The Hon'ble Supreme Court held that a constitutional amendment had to conform to the provisions of fundamental rights just like any other ordinary law. Accordingly, if the constitutional amendment violated any fundamental right, it was unconstitutional. Thereafter, a full Bench of thirteen Judges of the Supreme Court was constituted to consider the question of the validity of the Constitution (Twenty-Fourth Amendment) Act. The case directly raised the issue of amendability of fundamental rights. On 24 April 1973, the Supreme Court delivered its historic judgment in Kesavananda Bharati v. State of Kerala {AIR 1973 SC 1461} case. Six judges held that the power of amendment under Article 368 was plenary and was not subject to any implied and inherent limitations in respect of any matter, including fundamental rights. Six other judges and the CJI held that Parliament could not, in exercise of its amending power, destroy or damage the basic structure of the Constitution by altering the essential features of the Constitution and that fundamental rights were essential features of the Indian Constitution. Accordingly, a constitutional amendment which merely abridged a fundamental right with 'reasonable restrictions' was not unconstitutional, *but if it abrogated* a fundamental right, the Supreme Court would strike it down as unconstitutional. Hence, by a majority of one, the concept of an *unamendable basic structure* of the Constitution came into vogue. *This is our first pillar of Constitutionality.*

Thus, Part III consisting of Fundamental Rights became unamendable, and hence beyond any Parliamentary majority. Unless a revolution scraps the Constitution, it is now a permanent given in Indian affairs. The fundamental rights incorporated in Part III of the Indian Constitution have a close similarity to the Universal Declaration of Human Rights, 1948. During the course of the debates in the Constituent Assembly, members had also referred to the Universal Declaration of Human Rights. But in 1975, India experienced a threat to fundamental rights from a new angle-it's suspension. Prime Minister Mrs. Indira Gandhi claimed that the nation was threatened by internal disturbance and declared Emergency under Article 352. Part XVIII of the Indian Constitution deals with Emergency provisions that enable temporary suspension of fundamental rights. Article 352 had empowered the President to issue a Proclamation of Emergency if he was satisfied that a grave emergency existed whereby the security of India was threatened by war or external aggression or internal disturbance. Since this last expression was vague and liable to misuse as was in 1975-77, therefore by the Constitution (Forty-Fourth Amendment) Act, 1978 during the Janata Party rule, the expression 'armed rebellion' was substituted for the expression "internal disturbance." While a Proclamation of Emergency is in operation. Article 359 empowers the President to suspend the right to move any court for the enforcement of fundamental rights.

The Hon'ble Supreme Court in its judgment in ADM Jabalpur v. S. Shukia (AIR 1976 SC 1207) capitulated and held that right to life and personal liberty was suspended during the operation of the Proclamation of Emergency and during that period, the writ of *habeas corpus* is not available. Only Justice H.R. Khanna disagreed. The subsequent Janata Party Government of Morarji Desai reversed that the framers of the Constitution of India also seemed to be aware of the Hindu heritage of India. A perusal of the final copy of the Constitution, which was adopted by the Constituent Assembly on 26 November 1949, is most instructive in this regard. The Constitution includes twenty-two illustrations within its main body. These illustrations are listed at the beginning of the Constitution. The illustrations are apparently chosen to represent various periods and eras of Indian history. These illustrations have been selected to represent the ethos and values of India, which the Constitution seeks to achieve through its written words. The framers of the Constitution appear to have had no doubt in their minds that the Hindu heritage of this country is the ballast on which the spirit of the Constitution sails. The emphasis of these illustrations is on those symbols that encapsulate the most significant and authentic moments of a nation's history. The personality of Shri Rama, the enunciation of the Gita by Shri Krishna, the valour, humility and service of Shri Hanuman, the teachings of Bhagwan Buddha and Mahavira, the emphasis on academic pursuits symbolized by the Gurukul and the University of Nalanda. These images may not be said to exhaust the Hindu heritage, but they do capture the essential concerns of the Hindu mind: struggle against the evil forces, dedication to duty without passionate attachment, service and humility, compassion and charity, highest importance attached to learning and academic attainments, freedom to hold diverse opinions and viewpoints and an uncompromising spiritual eclecticism. These are the virtues that the Constitution seeks to visually represent and legally enforce without favour and fear. The Constitution, it was intended, to represent Hindu ethos.

The illustrations selected to represent the 'Muslim' period *also* imply this intention: Only two illustrations have been selected: (*i*) A portrait of Akbar and (*ii*) portraits of Shivaji and Guru Gobind Singh. From the whole range of Muslim themes, only Akbar is selected. Akbar come closest in his ideals and practices to what can be called the Hindu spirit: His relatively liberal politics, his reported refusal to make the Mughal state an instrument of exclusive Muslim hegemony, his relatively less hostile attitude towards Hindu religion, his refusal to treat Hindus as degraded dhimmis' on account of religious belief. Akbar approximated to a certain extent the Hindu ideal of social and political behavior and unsurprisingly found a place in the Constitution of India. The other two men who represent the 'Muslim Period' are Shivaji and Guru Gobind Singh: men who fought the persecution and bigotry of the Mughal rule under the successors of Akbar, especially Aurangzeb. Akbar is chosen because he was liberal: Shivaji and Gobind Singh are chosen because they fought the oppression and cruelty of the Mughal state which was acting as the instrument of Islamic religious supremacy. They refused to recognize a political dispensation that functioned as an instrument for the fulfillment of Islamic religious agendas. They fought for safeguarding the dignity of their culture and religious values from the depredations of a theocratic Muslim state. The three, Shivaji, Guru Tegh Bahadur, and Guru Gobind Singh represent the grand spiritual if secular, ethos of Hindutva. *The Constitution of India is cognizant of this fact. To this should have been added the Kings of Assam's Ahom Dynasty.* The pictures chosen from the British period and the era of India's freedom movement are also unique. The former era is represented by Tipu Sultan and Rani Lakshmi Bai, both inveterate warriors against European colonial domination, warriors whose battles were not defined in terms of mere speeches and slogans but enacted within the context of blood and sweat. Another figure chosen from the phase called 'Revolutionary movement for freedom' is Netaji Subhash Chandra Bose. One is compelled to ask the question: Why is Netaji chosen to represent the revolutionary movement for the freedom of India? The fact is that it was Netaji whose gallantry and dedication raised the morale of the freedom fighters and led to wider repercussion in other sections of Indian society. His courage, his sacrifice, his fighting spirit are the true values representative of the final assault of the Indian people on the edifice of colonial rule. The only person chosen to represent the theme 'India's Freedom Movement' is Mahatma Gandhi, whose deep association with Hindu values, Hind Swaraj and Ram Rajya are no hidden facts. The Constitution of India thus seems to have chosen the very Hindu icons to represent its ethos. The 'aroma' of Hinduness or Hindutva mindset also permeates the most important constitutional and administrative units of the Indian state. Nowhere is it more apparent than in the august premises of the Indian Parliament—a house where matters of national concern are discussed and the fate of the nation is decided. The head of the Lok Sabha is the Speaker, and what we find inscribed above the Chair of the speaker is the following: *Dharmachakra Pravartanaya* (for the turning of the wheel of righteousness). It is accepted by all that the notion of 'Dharma' is the most significant cultural signifier of the Hindu world. The rulers of ancient India had accepted the path of dharma as their area of political exertion and the managers of free India's politics accepted that notion by putting the *dharamachakra* on the national flag, and the related motto in the central place of the highest legislative body.

The Parliament of India bears prominent reminders of the prevailing nationally accepted Hindu ethos at many places:

(*i*) At door no. 1 is inscribed –
Lok Devarampatraarnu
Pashyema tvam vayam vera

[Open the door for the welfare of the people and show them the path of noble sovereignty]. Chhandogya

(*ii*) At the door of the Central Hall -
Ayam nijah paroveti ganana laghuchetasam
Udarcharitanam tu vasudhaivakutumbakam
[Panchantantra]

[To think in terms of 'me' and 'others' in a narrow say; for the men of liberal character the whole world is one family].

(*iii*) On the dome near lift no. 1 –
Na sa sabhayata na santi vriddhah
Vriddhah na to ye na vadantidharmam
Dharmah sa no yatra na satyamasti
Satyamna tadyachhalambhyupaiti [Mahabharat]

[No assembly is a sabha which does not comprise elders; he is not an elder who does not speak according to dharma; no dharma survives without truthfulness; and every truth is necessarily devoid of cunning and deceit].

(*iv*) On the dome near lift no. 2 –
Sabha v na praveshtaya
Vakavyam va samanjasam
Abruvan vibruvan vapi
Naro bluvati kilvishi [Manusmriti]

"Either do not enter the sabha, or if your do, speak only according to dharma when you are inside it. Those who do not speak or speak untruthfully and unrighteously are partakers of sin."

These teachings—and there are many more—inscribed on the domes and walls of the Indian Parliament signify the values that the fathers of Indian democracy and parliamentarianism wanted to inculcate. It goes without saying that all the noble virtues included in the above-mentioned aphorisms are derived from the Hindu heritage of India. The founding fathers seem to have found a deep consonance between India's Hindu ideals and the ideals of a modern secular democracy. The impact of Hindu heritage and its value systems on the legal and administrative life of India becomes all the more apparent when one examines the core ideals adopted by various institutions. Some of the examples are as follows:

(*i*) Government of India - *Satyameva Jayate*
(*ii*) Lok Sabha - *Dharmachakra Pravartanaya*
(*iii*) Supreme Court - *Yato Dharmastato Jayah*
(*iv*) All India Radio – *Bahujanhitaya*
(*v*) Doordarshan - *Satyam Shivam Sundaram*
(*vi*) Indian Army - *Seva Asmakam Dharmah*
(*vii*) Indian Navy - *Shan No Varunah*

(*viii*) Indian Air Force - *Nabhah Sprisham Diptam*

(*ix*) Delhi University - *Nistha Dhriti Satyam*

(*x*) Life Insurance Corporation of India - *Yogakshemam Vahamyaham*

These are ideals of the Hindu world. They do not convey religious dogmas; therefore, no rituals or gods are invoked in them; they are civilizational values whose sanction comes from deep humanism and a commitment to a righteous way of life. They are noble virtues whose adoption was deemed to be relevant for the future of modern India's democratic polity. The Indian Constitution and the Indian polity pay their homage to the ancient value systems of the Hindu way of life, and Hindutva. Thus, the interpretations of the higher judiciary of the land, assigning the Hindu way or Hindutva to the centuries old socio-cultural underpinnings of India are not an exercise of mere juristic interpretation. It is more fundamentally the acknowledgement of those social, cultural, ideational and political norms that give the people and territory of India their defining identity. Inspite of the currently fashionable denial by the purveyors of a warped secularism, the Hindu underpinning of India's milieu have been vested with great significance by the leaders of the freedom movement and has been subtly but insistently stated in the structures of the democratic institutions set up by Independent India. Our Constitution, our Parliament, our highest Judiciary, and other important organs of the state recognize most clearly that the ultimate normative sources of inspiration for shaping free India's destiny would remain the millennia old heritage of Hindu ideals and civilizational concerns. The founding fathers of India's political regime seem to have no doubt in their minds that India can remain a pluralistic and democratic polity only to the extent that it adheres to the fundamental values of a democratic, polyform and pluralistic Hindutva.

So, the question arises: Will Hindutva be a contradiction or violative of the Constitution? In other words, can Hindutva be incorporated by amending the present Constitution subject to the Basic Structure Rule?

We find from our research that most major Hindutva goals do meet the test of Constitutionality and hence need to be pursued even under the present Constitution. Of the decisions of the Hon'ble Supreme Court commonly referred to in this regard as "Hindutva decisions," the most important one is in *Manohar Joshi* [(1996)1 SCC 169]. In his election speeches Manohar Joshi, the winning Shiv Sena candidate had said that "[T]he first Hindu State will be established in Maharashtra." The High Court of Bombay set aside his election. But the Supreme Court restored Joshi's election observing that "a mere statement that the first Hindu State will be established in Maharashtra is by itself not an appeal for votes on the ground of his religion but the expression, at best, of such a hope."

The Court went much further and using the words "Hindu", "Hinduism" and "Hindutva" interchangeably observed that those terms were not amenable to any precise definition and no meaning in the abstract *would confine the term "Hindutva" to the narrow limits of religion alone.* The Court further observed, "[T]he term 'Hindutva' is "related more to the way of life of the people in the sub-continent. It is difficult to appreciate how in the face of [prior rulings] the term "Hindutva" or "Hinduism" per se, in the abstract, can be assumed to mean and be equated with narrow fundamentalist Hindu religious bigotry...." (p.159, para 37).

Rule of Law which is governance based on citizens' rights & duties, is structured in the Constitution of a nation while the enforcement mechanisms are based on procedures set out in the Constitution [e.g., Article 226 and 32 on Writs] and statutes consistent with it. The Courts provide as an independent judiciary, the interpretations of and direction to the State of the same by. In Hindu tradition, there is a highly sophisticated body of rules of interpretation and procedures prescribed in Jaimini's *Mimamsa* (in Sanskrit means "investigation") which sums up the general rules of *Nyaya.* Can we blend Mimamsa rules into the Constitution? Yes indeed. Recently, a Supreme Court judge Markandeya Katju in open court suggested the use of Mimamsa rules to fill the gaps in the traditional western Maxwell procedures in our courts.

Thus, Constitutionality consists of the *quality* of the statutes, of enforcement procedures of rights and the performance of duties, in conformity with the provisions and principles of the Constitution. This quality can be imbibed by us from the glorious Hindu texts of Mimamsa and Vedanta. In the name of modernity, defined as by our elite as anything Western, we have shown scant regard for our ancient tradition of legal argumentation. The Hon'ble Supreme Court on 18 December 2007 the UP State Agro Industrial Ltd case observed that the Mimamsa Rules of Interpretation (MRI) were still relevant and ought to be used in Courts alongside the traditional Maxwell Rules. Mimamsa Rules have been used by our *rishis,* since Jaimini wrote his Sutras, to resolve conflict betweeb various Smritis. The Supreme Court applied these Rules to classify "animal driven vehicles" in their judgment. A Bench of Justice Markandey Katju and Justice A.K. Ganguly in its order in another case said "It is deeply regrettable that in our Courts of law, lawyers quote Maxwell and Craies but nobody refers to the MRI. Most of today's lawyers would not have even heard of its existence. Today our so-called educated people are largely ignorant about the great intellectual achievements of our ancestors and the intellectual treasury which they have bequeathed us." The Bench said further: "the Mimansa Principles were our traditional system of interpretation of legal texts. Although originally, they were created for interpreting religious texts [pertaining to the Yagya sacrifice], gradually they came to be utilised for interpreting legal texts and also for interpreting texts on philosophy, grammar, etc. i.e. they became of universal application. Thus, Shankaracharya has used the *Mimansa adhikaranas in his bhashya* on the Vedanta sutras. There were hundreds of books [all in Sanskrit] written on the subject, though only a few dozen have survived the ravages of time, but even these shows how deep our ancestors went into the subject of interpretation."

The Mimansa or the Purva Mimansa Rules to be exact, were laid down by Jaimini in his *Sutras* written around 600 B.C. That they are very ancient is proved by the fact that they are referred to in many Smritis which themselves are very old. Thus, the Apastamba Sutras copiously refer to Jaimini's principles. Since these Sutras are written in very concise form it became necessary to explain them. Many commentaries were written on them, the main ones being of Sabara, who lived around Second Century A.D., and Kumarila Bhatta and Prabhakara, who lived around the Eighth Century A.D. Before mentioning some of the Mimansa Principles it is necessary to give a short background. Classical Hindu Philosophy has six schools (shatdarshan) all of which aim at Moksha (liberation). Purva Mimansa is one of these schools, and according to it one can achieve Moksha by performing Yagya (sacrifice) in accordance with the Shastras. The Shastras consist of Shruti and Smriti, the former being superior to the latter. Shruti consists of the four Vedas, the Brahmanas, the Aranyaks and the Upanishads. Brahmanas are treatises written in prosewhich prescribe methods of performing various Yagyas. To every Veda one or more Brahmanas are attached. Thus, the Aitareya Brahmana is attached to the Rig Veda, the Taitareya Brahmana to the Black Yajur Veda, the Shatapatha Brahmana to the White Yajur Veda, and the Tandya Brahmana to the Sama Veda. After Shankaracharya's historic victory over Mandana Misra, Purva Mimansa, as a philosophic system, declined in importance. Shankaracharya was a proponent of Uttar Mimansa (also known as Vedanta), according to which Moksha can be achieved by knowledge of Brahma. Shankaracharya preached that Jnanakanda (the Vedantic Path) is superior to Karmakanda (the performance of Yagya). He shifted the emphasis in the Shrutis from the Brahmanas to the Upanishads, and his view was accepted, and ever since Vedanta became the dominant school of Hindu philosophy. However, though Purva Mimansa lost prominence to Vedanta in Philosophy, its importance remained as paramount as before in the legal sphere. It must however be clarified that the Mimansaks were not jurists. Their aim was to perform the Yagya properly, for they sincerely believed that this was the means to achieve moksha. For the conduct of Yagyas in accordance with the rules they had to devise a system of interpretation to resolve the conflicts, ambiguities, etc. in the Shrutis, which were aggravated by the archaic, pre-Panini Sanskrit employed in the Vedic texts.

No doubt the principles of interpretation were initially evolved to resolve conflicts that arose in connection with the meaning of rules governing performance of the Yagya, but gradually these principles came to be accepted for interpreting legal texts also which were mixed up with religious rules in the Smritis. It was therefore natural that our great commentators like Vijnaneshwara, Jimutvahana, etc. had utilised these Mimansa principles whenever faced with any ambiguity or conflict in the various Shastras. Unfortunately, there has not been much effort to explain these principles. The advent of Anglo-Saxon Law coerced on us must have been responsible for this lack of study.

The Mimansa principles are in two respects superior to Maxwell's principles of interpretation, viz.: (1) They can be utilised not only for interpreting statutes but also judgments, whereas Maxwell's principles can only be used for interpreting statutory law, (2) They are more detailed and systematic. The Mimansa Principles distinguish between obligatory statements and non-obligatory statements. The main obligatory rule is called a Vidhi (or a Pratishedh, if it is in negative form). Vidhis are of 4 types as mentioned below:

(1) Utpatti Vidhi, or a substantive injunction (e.g. 'perform the agnihotra'),
(2) Viniyoga Vidhi, or applicatory rules (e.g. 'with curdled milk perform the agnihotra'),
(3) Prayog Vidhi, or rules of procedure, and
(4) Adhikara Vidhis (rules regarding rights and personal competence).

Apart from these Vidhis proper (mentioned above) there are also certain quasi Vidhis called niyamas and parishankhyas, but it is not necessary to go into details here. Vidhis are found in Brahmanas. The main non-obligatory statement is known as an Arthavada. An Arthavada is a statement of praise or explanation. Most of the Vedas proper consist of Arthavadas as much of the Vedic hymns are in praise of some god, and do not lay down any injunction. Arthavada is like the preamble or statement of objects in a statute. An Arthavada has no legal force by itself, but it is not entirely useless since like a statement of objects or preamble it can help to clarify an ambiguous Vidhi, or give the reason for it. Sometimes a Vidhi is also seen couched in the form of Arthavada. This situation has necessitated the need for evolving a system of interpretation. Six axioms of interpretation have therefore been developed for the interpretation of shastras.

By reason of the amendment of Article 359 of the Constitution by the Constitution (Forty-Fourth Amendment) Act, the provisions of Article 21 cannot now be suspended or derogated from even during an emergency. No court can hereafter rule that habeas corpus is not available during an emergency. The relationship of fundamental rights with the Directive Principles of State Policy in Part IV of the Constitution has been a subject of considerable and continuing debate. A division of fundamental rights into two categories—justiciable and non-justiciable—was recommended by the Sapru Committee as early as 1945. At the time of framing the Constitution, the Advisory Committee on Fundamental Rights recommended:

> "We have come to the conclusion that in addition to these fundamental rights, the Constitution should include certain directives of State Policy which, though not cognizable in any court of law, should be regarded as fundamental in the governance of the country."

Directive principles are not enforceable by any court but the principles laid down are, nevertheless, fundamental to the governance of the country and it is the duty of the State to apply these principles in making laws (Article 37). Part IV prescribes the goals or the ideals to be achieved by India as a Welfare State. Fundamental rights are the means for realizing these goals. At one stage there was a sharp controversy regarding the role of fundamental rights vis-a-vis directive principles. Early judicial thinking took the view that directive principles were subsidiary or subordinate to fundamental rights. The Constitution also prescribes the rights and duties of a citizen and it is the responsibility of the State to ensure the citizen gets his rights, as also encouraged to perform his duties as a part of the soft infrastructure of good governance.

The structure of our Constitution is consistent with the Hindu tradition, a part of Hindutva. Ancient Bharat or Hindustan was of *janapadas* and monarchs. But it was unitary in the sense that the concept of *chakravartin* [propounded by Chanakya], i.e., of a *sarvocch pramukh* or *chakravarti* prevailed in emergencies and war, while in normal times the regional kings always deferred to a national class of sages and *sanyasis* for making laws and policies, and acted according to their advice. This is equivalent to Art.356 of the Constitution. In that fundamental sense, while Hindu India may have been a union of kingdoms, it was fundamentally not a monarchy but a Republic. In a monarchy, the King made the laws and rendered justice, as also made policy but in Hindu tradition the king acted much as the President does in today's Indian Republic. The monarch acted always according the wishes and decisions of the court-based advisers, mostly prominent sages or Brahmins. Thus, Hindu India was always a Republic, and except for the reign of Ashoka, never a monarchy. Nations thus make Constitutions but Constitutions do not constitute nations.

Because India's Constitution today is unitary with subsidiary federal principles for regional aspirations, and the judiciary and courts are national, therefore the Rajendra Prasad-monitored and Ambedkar-steered Constitution—making, was a continuation of the Hindu tradition. *This is the second pillar of constitutionality for us—the Hindutva essence!* These aspects were known to us as our Smritis. Therefore, it is appropriate here to explore ways by which Hindutva can be blended into the present Constitution more explicitly. The Hindutva plank of restoring temples that were demolished by Islamic tyrants and mosques built on it, is constitutional thanks to the judgment in the Farooqui case. In this case [(1994) 6 SCC 360], the Constitution Bench has held that a mosque *is not an essential part of Islam and hence it can be demolished for a public purpose by a Government.* This opens the way for building a Ram temple in Ayodhya. Of course, the 1992 demolition of the Babri Masjid would have to be regarded as an offence under the IPC because of a mob taking law into its own hands. But the Babri Masjid demolition offence does not prevent a future Hindutva government from demolishing Masjids and Churches (also not an essential part of Christianity) built after demolishing Hindu temples. As the House of Lords U.K has held (1992) in the Nataraj idol case, because of *Prana prathista puja,* according to Agama Shastra, a temple is always a temple even if in disuse.

Thus, for restoring the Kashi Visvanath temple or the Krishna Janmabhoomi temple, demolishing of the existing mosques by a government is constitutionally permitted. Even in the Ramjanmabhoomi temple case currently entangled on the unauthorized demolition by some people taking law into their own hands, it is an IPC offence and has no constitutional significance. Any government can even now take-over the project for public good, and build a Ram Janma bhoomi temple.

Since the Article 44[1] is a Directive Principle for State Policy to have uniform *civil* code and moreover since the Muslims on ground of violation of the Shariat have not objected to a uniform *criminal* code which the Indian Penal Code is, hence it is constitutional to enforce Article 44 as not violative of Article 15, since the latter is subject to reasonable restrictions of health, morality and public order. The question whether India should adopt a uniform civil code should be treated as a legal question because it is a mandate addressed to the 'State' by Art.44 under Directive Principles of the Constitution. Unfortunately, in India, legal questions are politicized when it affects the "Muslim vote bank."

[1]Article 44 of the Constitution says –"The State shall endeavour to secure for the citizens a uniform civil code throughout the territory of India."

Chapter 5

Defalsified Hindu History

The facts of our history have to be well understood so that we are not condemned to re-live it. Our national identity has been deliberately distorted by a history written about us by invading aggressors. We have defined the Indian nation as "a nation of Hindus and those others who proudly acknowledge that their ancestors were Hindus."

What the current history textbooks today teach is still basically the theory of a few nineteenth-century European "scholars" (including the paid agent of the East India Company viz., Max Muller). According to them, around 1500 BC hordes of semi-barbarian, pastoral nomads, the so-called "Aryans," poured out of Europe/Central Asia into Northwest India, and drove south the ancestors of today's "Dravidians," then over a few centuries, they composed the Vedas, gradually got their "Aryan" culture (with its language, Sanskrit) to spread all over India, and eventually built the mighty Ganges civilization. This is so estimated because the Hindus valley layers so far excavated in the Mohenjodaro/Harappa ruins, show destruction from unnatural causes of a city civilization, to be around 1500 BC, while the Rig Veda talks of a pastoral society. Thus, pasting together, it means Vedic people destroyed the Indus Valley civilization. This, with some variations, is still today what the school-going child is taught. Not only textbooks, even respectable dictionaries and encyclopedias will tell you more or less the same thing.

However, today with new evidence tumbling out a debate rages not only in India but in Western universities and among eminent scholars and archaeologists. Many of them have in recent years called for a new look at this Aryan Invasion Theory (AIT). All of them agree that archaeological evidence entirely fails to support the Aryan invasion theory and actually goes against it; many of them also find the linguistic evidence that was used to buttress it, quite shaky. But this debate, as we shall see, is by no means limited to the academic world; it is not a dry scholarly matter, and it has far-reaching repercussions on today's India, especially where her unity and Identity is concerned. Such a "history" had been deliberately created by the British as a policy. Sir George Hamilton, Secretary of State for India, wrote on 26 March 1888 that *"I think the real danger to our rule is not now but say 50 years hence .... We shall (therefore) break Indians into two sections holding widely different views.... We should so plan the educational text books that the differences between community and community are further strengthened."*

After achieving independence, under the leadership of the Europeanized Jawaharlal Nehru and the implementing authority of the British set up ICS, revision of our history was never done. In fact, the very idea was condemned as "obscurantist" and Hindu chauvinist. The fabrication and falsification of our History begins with ancient India's chronology. The customary dates quoted for composition of the *Rig Veda* are: circa 1300 B.C., Mahabharata: 600 B.C., Buddha's *Nirvana:* 483 B.C., Maurya Chandragupta's coronation 324 B.C., and Ashoka: 268 B.C., These dates are entirely wrong. Those dates are directly or indirectly based on a selected reading of Megasthenes' account of India: 'Indika'. In fact, so much so that eminent British trained historians have called Indika the "sheet anchor of Indian chronology." The account of

Megasthenes has also an important bearing on distant questions such as the two-race (Aryan-Dravidian) theory, and on the pre-Vedic character of the so-called Indus Valley Civilization. Megasthenes was the Greek ambassador sent by Seleucus Nicator in c.302 B.C. to the court of the Indian king whom he and the Greeks called "Sandrocottus" stationed in "Palimbothra," the capital city of the kingdom. His son was called Sandrocruptus by Megasthanes. It is not clear how many years Megasthenes stayed in India, but he did write an account of his stay, titled *Indika.* The manuscript *Indika* is lost, and there is no copy of it available. However, during the time it was available, many other Greek writers quoted passages from it in their own works. These quotations were meticulously collected by Dr. Schwanbeck in the nineteenth century, and the compilation is also available to us in English (J.M. McCrindle: *Ancient India as Described by Megasthenes and Arrian*).

When European Indologists were groping clueless to date Indian history during the nineteenth century (after having arbitrarily rejected the various *Puranas*), the Megasthenes account came in very useful. These scholars simply identified "Sandrocottus" with Chandragupta, and "Palimbothra" with Pataliputra. Since Megasthenes talks of Sandrocottus as being a man not of "noble" birth who essentially usurped the throne from Xandrames and founded a new dynasty, the western writers took it as enough evidence to suggest that Sandrocottus was Chandragupta, who deposed the Nanda (=Xandrames) dynasty, and founded the Maurya dynasty. This identification, thus places Maurya Chandragupta circa 302 B.C. However, Megasthenes also notes that Sandrocottus was a contemporary of Alexander, and came to the throne soon after Alexander's departure. With a little arithmetic on how many days it would have taken Alexander to cross the Indus, etc., the scholars arrive at c.324 B.C. as the date of Chadragupta Maurya's coronation. *It is on this date that every other date of Indian history has been founded and re-constructed.* The western writers constructed other dates of Indian history by using the date on the number of years between kings given in the *Puranas,* even though they have generally discredited the Puranas. For instance, the Puranas give the number of years for the reign of Chandragupta and Bindusara as 62 years. Using this period, Asoka's coronation year is calculated by them as 324-62=circa 262 B.C.

This estimated year is then cross-checked and adjusted with other indicators, such as from the Ceylonese Pali tradition. The point that is being made here is that some of the important dates of Indian history have been directly determined by the identification of Megasthenes' Sandrocottus with Maurya Chandragupta, and Xandremes with Nanda. The founder of the Mauryas, however, *is not the only Chandragupta in Indian history*, who was a king of Magadh and founder of a dynasty. In particular, there is Gupta Chandragupta, a Magadh king and founder of the Gupta dynasty at Pataliputra. Chandragupta Gupta was also not of "noble" birth and, in fact, came to power by deposing the Andhra king Chandrasri. That is, Megasthenes', Sandrocottus may well be Gupta Chandragupta instead of Maurya Chandragupta (and Xandremes the same as Chandrasri, and Sandrocryptus as Samudragupta). In order to determine which Chandragupta, it is, we need to look further. It is, of course, a trifle silly to build one's history on this kind of tongue-gymnastics, but I am afraid we have no choice but to pursue the Megasthenes evidence to its end, since the currently acceptable but falsified history is based on it. In order to determine at which Chandragupta's court Megasthenes was ambassador, we have to look further into his account of India. We find he was at Pataliputra. We know from the *Puranas* (which are unanimous on this point) that all the Chandravamsa king of Magadh (including the Mauryas) prior to the Guptas, had their capital at Girivraja (or equivalently Rajgrha) and not at Pataliputra.

Gupta Chandragupta was the first king to have his capital in Pataliputra. This alone should identify Sandrocottos with Gupta Chandragupta. However, this point is a bit controversial because some 11th century A.D. sources call Pataliputra the Maurya capital, e.g., Vishakdatta in *Mudrarakshasa.* Pursuing Megasthenes' account further, we find most of it impossible to believe. He appears to be quite vague about details and is obviously given to the ancient Greek writers' weakness in letting his imagination get out of control. For example, "Near a mountain which is called Nulo there live men whose feet are turned backwards and have eight toes on each foot." [See *Solinus* 52.36-30 XXX.B]: "Megasthenes says a race of men (exist in India) who neither eat or drink, and in fact have not even mouths, set on fire and burn like incense in order to sustain their existence with odorous fumes...." (Plutarch, Frag.XXXI). However, Megasthenes appears to have made one precise statement of possible application which was picked up later by Pliny, Solinus, and Arrian. As summarized by Professor K.D. Sethna of Pondicherry, it reads:

"Dionysus was the first who invaded India and was the first of all who triumphed over the vanquished Indians. From the days of Dionysus to Alexander the Great, 6451 years reckoned with 3 months additional."

While there are a number of issues raised by this statement, the exactness with which he states his numbers should lead us to believe that Megasthenes could have received his chronological data from none else than the Puranic pundits of his time. To be conclusive, we need to determine who are the "Dionysus" of

Megasthenes' account. Traditionally, Dionysus (or Father Bachhus) was a Greek God of wine who was created from Zeus's thigh. Dionysus was also a great king, and was recognised as the first among all kings, a conqueror and constructive leader. There is a possible and credible Indian equivalent of Dionysus whom Megasthenes quickly equated with his God of wine.

Looking through the Puranas, one does indeed find such a person. His name is Prithu. Prithu was the son of King Vena. The latter was considered a wicked man whom the great sages could not tolerate, especially after he told them that the elixir soma should offered to him in prayer and not to the gods (Bhagavata Purana IV.14.28). The great sages thereafter performed certain rites and killed Vena. But since this led immediately to lawlessness and chaos, the *rishis* decided to rectify it by coronating a strong and honest person. The *rshis* therefore churned the right arm (or thigh; descriptions vary) of the dead body (of Vena) to give birth to a fully-grown Prithu. It was Prithu, under counsel from *rshi* Atri (father of *Soma*), who reconstructed society and brought about economic prosperity. Since he became such a great ruler, the *Puranas* have called him *adi-raja* (first king) of the world. So, did the Satapatha Brahmana (v.3.5 4.). In the absence of a cult of *Soma* in India, it is perhaps inevitable that Megasthenes and the other Greeks, in translating Indian experiences for Greek audiences, should pick on adi-raja Prithu who is "tinged with Soma" in a number of ways and bears such a close resemblance to Dionysus in the circumstances of his birth, and identify him as Dionysus. If we accept identifying Dionysus with Prithu, then indeed by a calculation based on the *Puranas* (done by D.R. Mankad, Koti Venkatachelam, K.D. Sethna, and others), it can be conclusively shown that indeed 6451 years had elapsed between Prithu and a famous Chandragupta. *This calculation exactly identifies Sandrocottus with Gupta Chandragupta and not with Maurya Chandragupta.*

This calculation must be necessarily long and tedious to counter the uninformed general feeling first sponsored by Western scholars, that the *Puranas* spin only fairy tales and are therefore quite unreliable. However, most of these people do not realize that most *Puranas* have six parts, and the *Vamsanucharita* sections (especially of Vishnu, Matsya, and Vagu) are a systematic presentation of Indian history especially of the Chandravamsa kings of Magadha. In order to establish these dates, I would have to discuss in detail the cycle of lunar asterisms, the concept of them according to Aryabhatta, and various other systems, and also the reconciliation of various minor discrepancies that occur in the *Puranas.* Constraints of space, however, prevent me from presenting these calculations here. On the basis of these calculations we can say that Gupta Chandragupta was "Sandrocottus" c.327 B.C. His son, Samudragupta, was the great king who established a unified kingdom all over India, and obtained from the Cholas, Pandyas, and Cheras their recognition of him.

Samudragupta also gave a beating of Seleucus Nicator, while his father Chandragupta was king. On this calculation we can also place Prithu at 6777 B.C. Derivation of other dates without discussion may also be briefly mentioned: Buddha's Nirvana 1807 B.C., Maurya Chandragupta c. 1534 B.C., Harsha Vikramaditya (Parmar) c. 82 B.C. Arun Bansal, who pioneered computer casting of horoscopes has, using astronomical data on planet positions given in the *Puranas,* determined that Lord Krishna was born on 21 July 3228 B.C and went back to his heavenly abode on 18 February 3102, when Kaliyug started. Western scholars accept the Puranic sequence of dynasty and Kings, so why not the dates? Instead

Western scholars have constructed an enormous edifice of dates to suit their contrived chronology of Indian history. A number of them are based on misidentification. For instance, the Rock Edict XIII, the famous Kalinga edict, is identified as Asoka's. It was, however, Samudragupta's. Samudragupta was a great conqueror and a devout admirer of Asoka. He imitated Asoka in many ways and also took the name Asokaditya. In his later life he too became a sanyasi or monk. The Ceylonese Pali traditions leave out the Cholas, Pandyas, and Cheras from the list of Asoka's kingdoms, whereas Rock Edict XIII includes them. In fact, as many scholars have noted, the character of Asoka from Ceylonese and other traditions is precisely (as R.K. Mukherjee has said) what does not appear in the principal edicts. Facts which directly contradict Westerners theories, they have rather flippantly cast aside. We state here only two examples of such facts: (1) Fa-hsien was in India and at Pataliputra c.410 A.D. He mentions a number of kings, but makes not even a fleeting reference to the Gupta Kingdom, even though according to European scholars he came during the height of their reign. He also dates Buddha at 1100 B.C. (2) A number of Tibetan documents place Buddha at 2100 B.C.

Thus, when we examine the accounts of ancient India as given in current history books still in use against the background of available data and the primary sources, we find a fundamental mismatch between scientific evidence and facts and historical theories propounded. As number of Indian scholars and institutions have begun to challenge the West-tutored falsified history. For example, Dr. N.S. Rajaram has admirably summarized this in his works debunking the bogus Aryan-Dravidian divide:

(*a*) There is no Indian archaeological record of any invasion and/or massive migration from Eurasia in the Vedic period.

If anything, we find traces of movement in the opposite direction—to West Asia and even Europe.

(*b*) The geography described in the Rigveda corresponds to North India in the fourth millennium BC and earlier and not Europe or Eurasia.

(*c*) The flora and fauna described in the Vedic literature, especially those found in the sacred symbols, are tropical and subtropical varieties and not from the temperate climate or the steppes.

(*d*) The climate corresponds to that found in North India.

The Aryan-Dravidian divide in the history taught in schools and universities is purely a conception of foreign historians like Max Mueller and has no basis in India historical records. This fraudulent history has been lapped up by many upper caste Indians, as their racial passport to Europe. Such has been the demoralization of the Hindu mind, which we have to shake off through a new factual account of our past History. But today, the bogus British imposed theory is being challenged by two new discoveries, one archaeological and the other linguistic. Firstly, in the Rig Veda, the Ganges, India's sacred river, is only mentioned once, but the mythic Saraswati is praised fifty times.

For a long time, the Saraswati river was indeed considered a myth, until the American satellite Landstat was able to photograph and map the bed of this magnificent river, which was nearly 14 km wide and took its source in the Himalayas. Archaeologist Paul-Henri Francfort, who studied the Saraswati region at the beginning of the Nineties, found out the Saraswati had "disappeared," because around 2200 B.C., an immense drought reduced the whole region to aridity and famine. "Thus," he writes, "most inhabitants moved away from the Saraswati to settle on the banks of the Indus and Sutlej rivers."

As the discovery of the Saraswati river, the decipherment of the Indus scripts also goes to prove that the Harappan civilization, of which the seals are a product, belonged to the latter part of the Vedic Age and had close connections with Vedantic works like the Sutras and the Upanishads.

Hence, it is becoming more and more clear that there never was an Aryan invasion in India, a theory which was imposed upon the subcontinent by its colonisers and is today kept alive by Nehruvian historians such as Romila Thapar missionaries (to convert the drowntrodden tribals and Dravidians, by telling them that Hinduism was a religion thrust upon them by the hated "Brahmin" invaders) and the Communists (who hate anything Hindu). But as long as India will not rewrite its history books and teach its children to be proud of its ancient and indigenous civilization, there will be others who will come and exploit India. Using the astronomy techniques following pivotal events of the Lord Ramayana at the following point in time:

Lord Rama's birth : 4 December 7323 B.C.,
Lord Rama's marriage with Sita : 7 April 7307 B.C.,
Lord Rama's exile : 29 November 7306 B.C.,
Hanuman's entry to Lanka : 1 September 7292 B.C.,
Construction of Setu (bridge) : 26-30 Oct. 7292 B.C.,
The beginning of the great war : 3 November 7292 B.C.
Ravana's killing by Lord Rama : 15 November 7292 B.C.
Lord Rama's return to Ayodhya : 16 November 7292 B.C.

As Dr. N.S. Rajaram has noted we now have the technical tools needed to unlock the secrets of our past, but it needs dedicated study and research in several disciplines. It is important, however, to familiarize oneself with the basics of human genetics to be able to make use of the wealth of ideas and data that are becoming available to historians. This calls for a new generation of historians that is more educated in science, as also less deferential towards anything handed down by Western academia. Humanities scholars in India need to catch up with the confidence developed by Indian scientists and technologists. Sri Aurobindo wrote seven decades ago that "Indian scholars have not been able to form themselves into a great and independent school of learning is due to two causes: the miserable scantiness of the mastery in Sanskrit provided by our universities, crippling to all but born scholars, and our lack of sturdy independence which makes us over-ready to defer to European [and Western] authority." How true it is even today!

Thus, the history of no free country can be structured on foreign accounts of it. The time has come for us to take seriously our Puranic sources and to imbibe a de-falsified and well-founded history of ancient India, a history written by Indians about Indians. Such a re-written history would bring out the amazing continuity of a nation, which nation asserted its identity again and again at times of war and political crises. It should focus on the fact that at the centre of our perception of Indian nation is the concept of the *Chakravartin* ideal—to defend the nation from external aggression while giving maximum internal autonomy to the *janapadas*.

A correct, defalsified history would record that Hindustan was conceptually one in the art of governance, in the style of royal courts, in the methods of warfare, in the maintenance of its agrarian base, and in the dissemination of information. Otherwise it was decentralized for autonomy of villages in self-administration. The Panchayat system is a manifestation of that.

The correct perception of Indian identity is we are a people who have always constituted a nation living in a geographical location spanning from Kashmir to Kanyakumari, from Cuttack to Car Nicobar, bound together in a continuing civilization of more than 10,000 years, a people who are mostly of Hindu religious faith or of those others of separate but equally respected faith, whose ancestry is however Hindu. A rudderless India so far, disconnected from her past has, as a consequence, become a fertile field for religious poachers and neo-imperialists from abroad who paint India as a mosaic of immigrants much like a crowd on a platform in a railway junction. That is, it is clandestinely propagated that India has belonged to those who forcibly occupied it and gave it an identity. This is the theme around which the Islamic fundamentalists and fraud Christian crusaders are again at work, much as they were a thousand years ago, but of course in new dispensations, sophistication, and media forms. The Hindu unity of India has to be seen from time immemorial. Sri Aurobindo never tired of stressing this essential unity:

> "In India," he said, "at a very early time the spiritual and cultural unity was made complete and became the very stuff of the life of all this great surge of humanity between the Himalayas and the two seas.

Sri Aurobindo also said:

> *"A time must come when the Indian mind will shake off the darkness that has fallen upon it, cease to think or hold opinions at second and third hand and reassert its right to judge and enquire in a perfect freedom into the meaning of its own Scriptures. When that day comes we shall, I think, {.....} question many established philological myths—the legend, for instance, of an Aryan invasion of India from the north, the artificial and inimical distinction of Aryan and Dravidian which an erroneous philosogy has driven like a wedge into the unity of the homogenous Indo-afghan race."*

This intrinsic Hindu unity has thus been sought during the last two centuries to be undone by legitimizing such bogus concepts as Aryan-Dravidian racial divide theory, or that India as a concept never existed till the British imperialists invented it, or that Indians have always been ruled by invaders from abroad. Thus, the concept of intrinsic Hindu unity, and India's Hindu foundation are thus dangerously under challenge by these forces. Tragically most Hindus today are not even cognizant of it. Thomas Babington Macaulay who vowed that by change in India's educational system he would create a class of Indians in blood and color, but English in taste, in opinions, in morals, and intellect, has eminently succeeded. The Hindutva movement based on Vedantic principles must undo this erroneous and dysfunctional assimilation. Another deliberate misrepresentation of Indian history by the British was of the First War of Independence which the British re-named disparagingly as "Indian Mutiny."On 10 May 1857, Indian soldiers of the regiments stationed at Meerut (U.P.) killed their British officers, marched to Delhi and liberated the city from British control. They then proclaimed the 82-year-old Bahadur Shah Zafar as the "Emperor of Hindustan." The Emperor then appointed a Hindu as his 'Prime Minister' Mukund Ram just as Nana Saheb Baji Rao, the adopted son of the Peshawas and partner in the revolt, appointed a Muslim, Azimullah as his 'Prime Minister'. At Red Fort, the Bhagwa Dhwaj (saffron flag) was unfurled.

The uprising did not last long. In Delhi it was over by September 1857, and the domino effect in the country as a whole of the revolt was contained by end 1858. But the popular uprising fired the imagination of the nation and from the ashes of the burnt-out revolution, sparks continued to ignite revolt in the country till Mahatma Gandhi led the nation finally to

Freedom in 1947. Exactly 160 years later today, however, the whole of India has become oblivious of this historic date and of the event that was the forerunner of India's freedom. No meetings, no TV discussions, no resolutions for this revolutionary day in a country which is ready to celebrate or mourn anything or anybody. During the UPA reign, even for a Pope in faraway Vatican we mourned for three days when the rest of the world except Italy did not see it fit to do so. We forgot 10 May 1857 because we were programmed since then for nearly a century to delete it from our collective memory. After achieving Independence in 1947, the amnesia was not cured by Free India's government. The British imperialists who understood the significance and import of the 1857 uprising, had ensured that it be ridiculed and downgraded as a "Sepoy mutiny," as a sporadic and limited uprising of soldiers that was ignited due to obscurantist reasons such as aversion to 'pig fat' in the cartridges. Not only the Imperialists, but the Marxist thinkers as well sought to play it down as a 'reaction'. Writing in New York Daily Tribune in a series of articles in 1857, Karl Marx termed it as an army revolt, "a military mutiny" but of national proportion only because "the natives' apprehension" that Government may otherwise interfere with their religion.

It was much later in 1957 a hundred year later that Marxist writer P.C. Joshi corrected the perspective of the party line. Others like Sir John Kaye, a prolific scribe, wrote that 1857 was due to the "fear on part of the Brahmins of the social changes" introduced by the British! It was Veer Savarkar however who in 1909 challenged this diminution and degradation of the 1857 uprising. He wrote his account of 1857 under the title "The Indian War of Independence: 1857." It was printed in Holland, but nevertheless the British authorities proscribed it. Savarkar re-interpreted 1857 as a war of independence, and his magnum opus served to fire the imagination of the youth for years to come till 1947. Savarkar's contribution to nation building by his well-researched and scientific analysis of 1857 uprising the First War of Independence shall remain everlasting and deserving of a Bharat Ratna. Only those brain washed by the British Imperialist can devalue it or detract from its seminal character. Savarkar saw the 1857 uprising as a national spirit that aroused "sepoy and civilian, king and pauper, Hindu and Mahomedan" to a revolution. In his book the Indian War of Independence of 1857, he asks:

> "What, then were the real causes and motives of this revolution? What were they that for them men by the thousand willingly poured their blood year after year? What were they that Maulvis preached them, learned Brahmins blessed them that for their success prayers went up to Heaven from the mosques of Delhi and the temples of Benares?" And he answered this question as "These great principles were Swadharma (one's duty) and Swaraj {self-government}."

Savarkar approvingly quotes the newly installed 'Emperor of Hindustan's Proclamation' as stating:

> "Hindus and Mohamedans of India! Arise! Brethern arise! Of all the gifts of God, the most gracious is that of Swaraj. God does not wish that you should remain idle. He has inspired in the hearts of Hindus and Mohamedans the desire to turn the English out of our country."

Thus, Savarkar credits Nana Sahib, Bahadur Shah Zafar, Rani of Jhansi, and Khan Bahadur Khan of Rohilkhand along with the priests (Brahmins and Maulvis) of forcefully attempting a national consciousness of Hindustan to liberate the nation from foreigners. The Hindustan, a term used by both Hindus and Muslims even today to describe India, would be 'Swadesh' for both Hindus and Muslims. Savarkar explains this adherence to the concept of Hindustan as follows:

> "As long as the Mohamedans lived in India in the capacity of rulers, so long, to be willing to live with like brothers was to acknowledge national weakness. Hence, it was up to then, necessary to consider the Mahomedans as foreigners."

Naturally no Muslim ruler adopted a secular state, and in fact adopted discriminatory taxes based on religion. Conversion to Islam was carried out by force, coercion and cruelty as evidenced in the tribulation suffered by Guru Teg Bahadur. So where was the question of brotherhood?

Savarkar then holds that after the heroism of Guru Gobind, Rana Pratap and the Maharattas, that grievance was no more valid, and that the original distinction between the Hindus and Muslims "must be laid to eternal rest."

Both communities, he adds in his magnum opus, are children of the soil of Hindustan, children of the same Mother India and of the same blood. He exhorted all to "create a passionate desire in the Hindustan for this ideal, and make all the country to rise simultaneously for the purpose of achieving it."

The 1857 spirit and the magnificent articulation of it by Veer Savarkar stood with us in good stead throughout the Freedom Struggle. It was ultimately derailed and destroyed by one "Himalayan Blunder" and two acts of treachery. The blunder was the Khilafat Movement of Mahatma Gandhi which he himself acknowledged as his Himalayan Blunder. That was by opposing the modernizing secular movement of Kamaal Ataturk in Turkey, Gandhi dignified reactionary conservative movement amongst Muslims of India, and rethroned the concepts of Darul Islam {Muslim ruled states} and Darul Harab (Muslims in violent rebellion in non-Muslim ruled states) in large enough measure in the Muslim mind. But it was the betrayal of Jawaharlal Nehru of the 1937 Lucknow electoral pact with Khaliq uz Zaman of the Muslim League that shocked the Muslims especially those Muslims who had wanted to be partners with Hindus in the Freedom Movement [by acknowledging that they were both children of Mother India seeking to liberate her]. Nehru wriggled out of a pre-election agreement with the Muslim League to share in power in the UP Government after finding that Congress party had won majority on its own. This betrayal of a written pact swung emotional Muslims to demand Pakistan for the first time in 1940 at the Lahore session of the Muslim League. Nehru again in 1946 by addressing a provocative press conference in Bombay sabotaged all efforts by Gandhi to affect a transfer of power from the British without Partition. Pakistan became a certainty that day, and the Hindu-Muslim brotherhood which flowered from 1857 onwards was subverted and finally laid to rest in 1947. The framework for Hindu-Muslim brotherhood that Savarkar so brilliantly set-out in the War of Independence 1857 hence, can be revived. At some later date after the menace of Pakistani terrorism is sorted out finally. Till then we must celebrate 10 May 1857 as equal to, if not more than 15 August 1947. The threat from the Feringhi {foreigner} is today as real as in 1857 and the nation must unite for it, without any appeasement or compromise on the ancient roots of Hindustan.